spiritual realities

Volume 4

POWERS AND ACTIVITIES OF MAN'S SPIRIT

by
Harold R. Eberle

Winepress Publishing
Yakima, Washington, USA

Spiritual Realities, Volume IV:
Powers and Activities of Man's Spirit

© 1998 by Harold R. Eberle

Winepress Publishing
P.O. Box 10653
Yakima, WA 98909-1653
1-800-308-5837
(509-248-5837 from outside the USA)

Library of Congress Catalog Card No. 97-060374
ISBN 1-882523-12-1

Cover by Jeff Boettcher
Graphic Art by Eugene M. Holmes

Unless otherwise stated, all biblical quotations are
taken from the *New American Standard Bible* ©
1977, The Lockman Foundation, La Habra, Califor-
nia 90631.

Dedication and Thanks

This book would not have been possible if it had not been for Pastor Jim Leuschen of Spokane, Washington, who helped me think through the many doctrinal issues and challenged me on numerous points. His theological insight brought me back down to earth and forced me to communicate spiritual principles in understandable terms.

Also, I had input and editing advice from Peter Eisenmann, Dennis Jacobson and Annette Bradley. Each of these have left their mark on these pages.

Table Of Contents

Introduction

The Christian faith declares that we have
more to our being than just a physical body.
There is an invisible, spiritual side to our nature.
Although all Christians accept this fact, few have
dared to consider the implications. Let's be dar-
ing.

In Volume II, we laid out the fundamentals of
man's nature. In addition to the physical body,
we investigated the invisible side and discovered
that it consists of two elements, a soul and a
spirit.

Spirit   Soul   Body

We saw the soul as superimposed over the
physical body, having the same shape and size.
The spirit, we learned, is the flowing energy
within. This energy sustains life within the soul

and within the physical body (Job 34:14-15). It also acts as a light, quickening our thoughts and allowing us to think (I Cor. 2:11). The spirit of man is the invisible energy circulating and flowing within as a river from our heart (Prov. 4:23).

Spirit/Soul/Body

The spirit of man originated with the first breath God breathed into Adam. That spiritual substance is passed through the generational lines. Because the spirit of man has its source in God, it is spiritual in nature, and therefore, is not limited by natural laws. This *God-stuff* in us has supernatural properties. The implications of this are profound.

As we delve into these subjects, keep in mind that all human beings, Christians and non-Christians, have spiritual energy flowing within them. There is a difference, however, between the spirit of the Christian and that of the non-Christian. Through sin, people experience spiritual death. However, when a person places their faith in Jesus Christ, they receive a fresh injection of God's life. Jesus explained that the rivers flowing within the believer would be rivers of "living" water (John 7:37-39). Every human being has a spirit that sustains his life and flows like energy, but only the believer has a spirit which has been made alive by a fresh injection of God's life (Rom. 8:10).

To see these basic concepts developed from a biblical perspective, I refer you back to Volume II. Proceeding from here, we now will study how the spirit of man can reach beyond his physical body to touch and influence both the natural and the spiritual worlds.

Spiritual Presence

The spirit not only flows within man, but it emanates out beyond the confines of the human body. Consider how this works.

The first outer manifestation of this spiritual energy is upon the countenance of a person. The Bible refers to this in several passages, especially in respect to people focusing their attention upon God. For example in Psalms 34:5, we are told:

> They looked to Him and
> were radiant,
> And their faces shall never
> be ashamed.

Moses approached the people after having talked with God; his face shone so brightly that he had to put a veil over it (I Cor. 3:13). In the Old Testament times, the Jewish women were noted for their increased beauty as they came out from the presence of God. On the negative side, we can read how Cain's countenance had noticeably fallen after he committed the murder of his brother (Gen. 4:6-7).

These countenance changes are due in part to changes in the flow of spiritual energy within a person. The spirit of man responds to the presence of God. It is also true that when people are full of life, there is a *spiritual brightness* about them. When the channel of the soul is opened, the life-energy within a person flows out, and it becomes tangibly evident.

Most people have observed this phenomenon in relation to the beauty of another individual. At times a person may exude an undeniable "glow." A husband may look at his wife and to him she appears to be "without spot or wrinkle." A young man may be mesmerized by the captivating beauty of a certain woman. As two single people catch each other's eyes, they may feel an energy radiating between them. In such situations, we discover that beauty is not just a function of natural features, but also the result of spiritual dynamics between people. (Read more about this in my book, *Two Become One.*)

Some researchers today claim to have observable evidence of energy surrounding every single person. Some of these studies are not as scientific as others, and we do not want to accept all as being equally reliable. However, the existence of this energy is undeniable. There have been many attempts, using modern technology, to photograph the energy fields surrounding individuals. Kirlian photography is most noted for the related studies, and, although Christians must not be gullible in believing everything being taught, there is some scientific data indicating an energy field around every living human body.

We must understand that scientifically-based techniques do not measure directly the spiritual energy, because spiritual things cannot be perceived by natural methods. What is happening is that the spiritual energy is influencing the natural elements in the atmosphere surrounding a person. The instruments being used measure in some way *the effects of the spiritual energy upon the natural elements.* This is an important fact in our understanding of how the spiritual world influences the natural.

Those who are or have been involved in various occult and mystical groups have proceeded beyond actual facts and have developed numerous teachings concerning this emanating energy. Typically, they talk about "auras" surrounding people and how various colors in people's auras mean certain things about their lives. Of course, Christians today may hesitate in using terms coined by those with evil interests, but the Bible-believer need not deny the existence of this spiritual energy. God is the one who breathed spiritual substance into man, and the Bible teaches us clearly that it flows outward as rivers from a person's innermost being.

This spiritual energy not only changes the countenance of a person, but it also emanates out from all human beings and surrounds them. A *spiritual presence* envelops every person and it can be sensed by others. You can identify this when someone sneaks up behind you. Usually, it is not very long until you "feel" them. The reality of such a presence beyond the confines of the human body can be seen in many situations of life, and even studied.

A related phenomenon can be observed when a thief breaks into a person's home during the night, and the homeowner awakens with a feeling of fear or apprehension. Such experiences only can be explained with an acceptance of the spiritual dynamics occurring between people.

Even more amazing are the responses stimulated in people who are being watched. For example, think of two strangers sitting at different tables in a restaurant. If one stares at the other without the second knowing it, sooner or later the second is likely to turn to see who is looking. Most people have experienced such spirit contact responses in some situation of their lives.

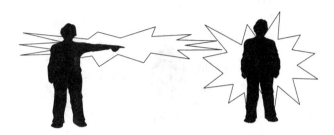

The spiritual presence surrounding and given off by a person is unique to that person and it influences other people in specific ways. For example, when a person is very angry, there is a tangible energy given off by them that causes others to be cautious when approaching. At other times, a person may have a very calm, gracious heart emitting a flow of peace to others. Even animals can sense this, as we can see when a house cat crawls into the lap of a relaxed individual. The experienced hunter knows that if he takes on a peaceful and confident attitude, wild animals will be less likely to detect him. In relationships between people, some individuals send out "sexual vibes" that let others know they are interested in certain wrong relationships. When a person is in self-pity, others around may feel the individual trying to draw attention to himself. People with arrogant attitudes project spiritual energy that can make others feel inferior. Some people emit spiritual energy that brings joy and happiness. All human beings have spiritual energy emanating from them, and that energy reflects the personality, purpose, and authority of the individual.

It is essential that you remember that the springs of life flow from the heart of man (Prov. 4:23). Therefore, heart-felt motivations and desires have much to do with the strength and character of the spiritual energy flowing out of an individual. Where a person directs his heart, that is where the spiritual energy within him flows. The strength of that flow is determined much by the decisions made deep within. The focus of one's entire being toward specific goals is as powerful and important as having agreement throughout a person's being with no confusion or indecision. In earlier volumes, we have discussed these and other characteristics which determine the strength of the spiritual flow. We do not need to repeat those discussions here but only refer to them, and then add to our understanding the following determining factor.

The *acceptance of personal responsibility* also determines the flow of spiritual energy from a person. We can see this when we talk about the spiritual presence surrounding an individual. Every person develops a sense of ownership over the area just around them. If a stranger suddenly stepped two inches in front of your face, you probably would be offended, and you would be right in asking, "What are you doing in *my* space?" The truth is that you have accepted responsibility and demanded authority over the space right around your body. Different people establish different limits to *their space*. Even in different cultures of the world and in different socioeconomic classes, people are taught to claim a certain amount of area around themselves. That of which they take possession in their heart becomes the area of their spiritual presence. A loved one may be allowed to step inside, but others must be invited. It is a reality of how we are made and how we live.

Keep these principles in mind: *the orientation of one's heart and the acceptance of personal responsibility determines the spiritual flow from one's innermost being.* This will have great implications as we continue to develop a biblical perspective concerning the flow of spiritual energy from our innermost being.

Beyond the Body

It is no more difficult for the spirit of a man to reach across town than it is for his spirit to touch the person sitting next to him. It requires no more energy nor any more determination on the part of the individual. Compare it with natural vision. It is no harder to look at the stars in the sky than it is to look at the paper in front of you. You can turn your attention toward things far away as easily as you can focus upon something near. In the same way, the spirit of a man can reach to any distance without effort.

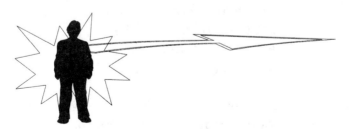

For evidence of this, consider what the Bible teaches us about our spiritual relationship to

Jesus. Even now our Lord is sitting at the right hand of the Father in heaven. His glorified body is located there, and His soul is also there associated with His body positioned in heaven. It is His spirit which extends from His being and reaches down to us: "...God has sent forth the Spirit of His Son into our hearts..." (Gal. 4:6). The body and soul have a set location but our Lord's spirit is not limited in that way.

In a similar manner, the Christian's spirit reaches out from his earthly vessel and into heaven (even though we cannot say exactly *where* heaven is). We know that our bodies and souls are located here upon this earth, but the Bible tells us that we are seated with Christ in heavenly places (Eph. 2:6). It is the *spirit* of the Christian which emanates out of his body and reaches even into the throne room of God.

This truth concerning the spirit reaching out of our bodies is related in many other Bible passages also. In Colossians 2:5, the Apostle Paul wrote to the early believers:

> For even though I am absent in body, nevertheless I am with you in spirit,... (Col. 2:5).

In verses such as this one, Paul referred to being in one location physically and in another in spirit (e.g., I Cor. 5:3-4; I Thes. 2:17).

Are we to believe these verses literally?

What we are about to discuss is difficult for many Christians to accept, especially those trained with a Western mind-set. As we explained in earlier volumes, those programmed to the Western way of thinking tend to view life from a very natural perspective: *natural things cause natural results.* Christians with a mind fixated along natural lines tend to read verses like Colossians 2:5 and just skip over them or excuse them as figures of speech. They have no place to put the idea that one's spirit could be located in a different place than their body. All Christians admit that man has an invisible side to his being, but if their minds are programmed along natural lines, they will tend to stop at that point and refuse to consider the spiritual implications of this principle.

What we discover is that Christians with a Western way of thinking may firmly state that they believe the Bible, but in reality they consciously or unconsciously make excuses to explain away what the Bible actually states. The truth is that the men used by God to write the Bible were not confined to any naturally-based Western mind-set (nor were they limited to an Eastern way of thinking). Therefore, if we want to understand what they wrote, we must open our minds to the whole realm of spiritual things. A Christian free of modern-day fixations is able to believe literally such Bible passages as Colossians 2:5 and, therefore, can begin to understand what Paul actually meant.

What, then, did Paul mean when he said he was absent bodily but with the Colossian Christians in spirit? Well, let's dare to take him literally. While Paul was writing those words he was physically in one location, but his spirit was reaching out of his body and actually was present with the Christians in the city of Colosse.

We can read an even more revealing example of this phenomenon in II Kings 5. There we learn how the Prophet Elisha was used by God to heal Naaman, the leper. Elisha would receive no gift for this great blessing, but afterward Elisha's servant, named Gehazi, secretly went to Naaman to receive gifts for himself. After Gehazi returned with the gifts, the Prophet confronted him, saying:

> "Did not my heart go with
> you, when the man turned
> from his chariot to meet
> you?" (II Kings 5:26a)

The Prophet knew what evil deed his servant had done. Without being present physically, he still was made aware spiritually. Elisha explained this by saying that his heart had gone with his servant.

We can understand such Bible passages only if we accept the truth that wherever a person's heart is pointed, that is where his spirit flows. Because the spirit is of the spiritual dimension, it is limited neither in space nor by distance the way that natural things are limited in this natural world. Your spirit goes in the direction of your love, faith, and hope. It also extends over that for which you accept personal responsibility. The heart determines the extent and direction of your *spiritual reach.*

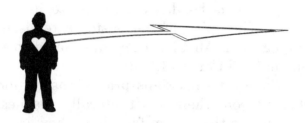

Realize that it is the spiritual substance—the energy, the divine breath, the residue of God's stuff in us—that reaches out of our bodies and goes where our heart is pointed. At this point in your thinking, separate the soul from the spirit (if needed, refer back to Volume II, Chapters 1 and 2). It is not the soul which emanates from the physical body. The soul can leave in other circumstances, and we will learn about those later, but here we are talking about the spiritual energy within a person emanating out of their soul and out of their body, and then reaching to another place.

Also, for clarification, we need to point out that not *all* of one's spirit leaves his soul/body. If that happened the person would die because there would not be enough spiritual energy left in the body or soul to maintain life (Job 34:14-15).

Instead, we understand that the spiritual energy is emanating outward and simply extending to the place to which it is directed.

Do not think of this as some mystical, rare experience. We believe that your spirit is touching all the people you love right now. A parent's spirit reaches out to his or her children. A married person is bonded spiritually to his or her spouse. The spirit of the pastor extends to his congregation. All Christians are joined together spiritually (I Cor. 12:12-13).

Whenever Christians pray earnestly for another person, their spirit literally reaches out and touches the person for whom they are praying. If Sister Suzie prays for her friend in a hospital across the country, Suzie's spirit may reach across the distance, and spiritual energy then may be imparted into that person. When we pray for our leaders, we literally release strength into them. When a father prays for his children, he increases the flow of his spirit to them.

It is helpful to distinguish between a person praying *to* God and a person directing his or her heart *toward* the person for whom he or she is praying. In our example of Sister Suzie praying for her friend in a distant hospital, we could ask whether her spiritual energy is being directed upward or toward the hospital. The answer may be *both*...both can and do happen. Later we will address when such directional forces are used rightly and wrongly, but here we recognize that both may be activated.

The human spirit (apart from the added strength of God) is limited. No one can send their spirit over all the earth or reach out to all people. Only to the degree that we love, accept responsibility, and have faith can we extend our spiritual strength to others. This limited nature of our spirit has many consequences.

For example, a certain missionary (whom we will call Bill) may work for an extended period in another land. During that time, he bonds with the people with whom he is laboring. Bill's spirit then abides with those people. If he leaves his mission field and returns to his homeland for a visit, Bill may find his heart still directed toward the people to whom he has given his life. As a consequence, he may be in one land physically while his spirit is reaching out to a distant location, just as Paul described. He may find himself, however, becoming exhausted spiritually. The result of his spiritual energy remaining in part with those on the foreign field can hinder his activities in his present location. We have seen missionaries in such conditions become physically ill and mentally unable to make even simple decisions. In such cases, we understand that they may not have enough spiritual substance left in their body/soul to function successfully.

Such symptoms are very common, and even the zealous Christian who goes overseas for a short missionary visit can experience a similar division of his spirit if he bonds with the people there. Typically, such a person will not be able to function at his peak back in his homeland until a period of time has passed. The process can be accelerated by a conscious act of the person forcefully directing his heart to where he is located physically. Also, it helps for him to engage in activities which he thoroughly enjoys, hence captivating his heart and redirecting it.

Related problems are not restricted to the missionary or the Christian. Every human being has a spirit that goes where his heart is directed. A military man may experience this phenomenon when he returns home from an overseas trip. The truck driver who loves being on the road gradually makes his home in his truck, and he extends his spirit wherever he goes. As a consequence, it is typical for truck drivers to have a terrible time ever being comfortable in one place or trying to settle down and change their lifestyles. Traveling salesmen, politicians campaigning on the road, itinerant preachers, etc., all experience similar problems.

Notice that it is not only the heart of love that extends a person's spirit outward, but also a *heartfelt sense of responsibility*. Paul wrote about his spiritual presence wherever he had sown the gospel and continued to hold influence. A pastor who accepts responsibility before God for his congregation—whether he realizes it or not—will emit his spirit out to his sheep. The spirit of a responsible parent abides upon his or her children. A coach who accepts responsibility for his team will influence his players with his own

spiritual energy. A businessman who accepts personal responsibility extends his spirit throughout
his business. This also has dark implications. Our Lord
Jesus said, "If therefore the light that is in you is
darkness, how great is the darkness!" (Matt.
6:23b). Such things as hate, prejudice, fear, etc.,
also can emanate to others. Although we do not
want to spend much time discussing the negative
aspects of this phenomenon, we recognize that
they are real and can work in all of our lives.

Our Communication
And Discernment

At this point we need to discuss our communication with each other. I am trying to convey spiritual principles which typically are not taught in most churches today. In this endeavor, we have many obstacles to overcome.

First and foremost is that of communication. The Apostle Paul explained in the Bible that spiritual concepts are foolishness to the natural mind (I Cor. 2:14). Because of this, it is very easy to be misunderstood. Since I am communicating through the written word and not face-to-face, I am trying to be very clear in my explanations and illustrations. Even at that, some ideas still may be taken wrongly.

Let me reassure you at this point that I have no intention of teaching things contrary to the Bible. If you knew me personally, you would know my heart and my convictions concerning the truth of God's Word. Some of the concepts we discuss may be unfamiliar to you, and some may seem even a little "too far out there," but please give me the benefit of the doubt and study the Bible for yourself to see whether or not these make sense as we discuss them further. Be as the noble-minded Bereans who studied the Word of God for themselves to see if the new things they were being taught were true or not (Acts 17:11).

Another obstacle we face in our communication involves the terminology we must use. The Apostle Paul faced this problem and explained that spiritual thoughts must be conveyed with spiritual words (I Cor. 2:13). I cannot explain how the spiritual world operates using everyday words such as "car," "gravity," "noise," "rocks," etc. The spiritual world does not consist of natural elements, and it does not operate according to natural laws. Jesus had to explain many spiritual principles using parables to which people could relate. Paul talked about his difficulty in communicating on such subjects because of the spiritual nature involved (I Cor. 2:14-3:3). If we are going to communicate effectively, we must use terms that accurately convey spiritual principles. Readers may not be familiar with some of these terms. We do not want to make people uncomfortable, but it is imperative that we communicate openly and effectively.

Unfortunately, evil men and women who have been involved in various occult practices have used spiritual terminology freely for years. As a consequence, they tend to *take possession* of those terms, and Christians become afraid to use them for fear of association.

For example, the symbol of the rainbow has been adopted by the New Age Movement, and a Christian today would risk being misunderstood if he had a bumper sticker on his car with a rainbow on it, regardless of the fact that God is the one who created the rainbow and gave it to us as a sign of His promise never again to destroy the earth by flood.

Consider the terminology, "out-of-body experience." Such terminology has come to be associated with evil occult practices, and a Christian teacher who uses these words in many Christian circles today will have to battle with resistance and fears that immediately arise in the minds of the listeners. He will likely be accused of heresy, misinterpretation of Scripture, dabbling in the occult and/or New Age Movement, or worse. However, the truth is that this terminology originates in the Bible. It was the Apostle Paul who explained how he was taken up into heaven, and he was not sure whether it was "in the body" or "out of the body" (I Cor. 11:2-3). I will talk more about such experiences later, but the point I am trying to make here is that I cannot communicate effectively with you unless you allow me to use spiritual terminology. Check yourself at this point: Does my use of the terminology, "out-of-body experience," cause you to be cautious of what I am about to say, or does it create in you an eagerness to learn spiritual principles expressed in the Bible? Your own preconceived ideas either will close or open your eyes and ears.

Let me assure you again that we are not going to teach any occultic, mystical error or heresy. Our textbook is the Bible.

However, I repeat, in order to teach spiritual principles, I must use spiritual words. I am asking you to set aside any limited associations you may have attached to these terms and honestly investigate the Scriptures with me. We are not borrowing terminology from evil men. Nor are we promoting their definitions of such words. We only are attempting to understand concepts which actually are taught in the Bible.

What we must overcome is the tendency to judge on the basis of comparisons with evil rather than with the Word of God. As we explain spiritual truths, do not slip into a carnal mindset which tends to analyze things on the basis of what something "sounds like." For example, concerning the common Charismatic experience of speaking in tongues, I have heard some Christians reject this gift on the basis that "it sounds like something primitive people in jungles do." Such judgments are not made on the basis of whether or not tongues is in the Bible, but rather on the basis of their *sounding like* something which the individual already has judged as evil. Thinking in such terms is limiting and leads to error.

When teaching on the spiritual dimension, I sometime hear people comment: "It sounds occult," or, "It sounds too mystical," or, "It sounds like New Age teaching." All such judgments may seem reasonable because we, as Christians, reject those deceptions. However, our standard should be the Bible. It is irrelevant, therefore, whether a specific teaching may or may not sound like anything you have heard before. So what? The important question is, "Is it taught in the Bible?"

Christians sometime are blinded to spiritual realities because they cannot see beyond previous judgments which they have made about things— judgments that clearly are wrong. Please, do not make this mistake. What I am asking you to do is to judge the things we will discuss, relying upon the Bible as your guide.

Let me give you a test here. Would negative feelings start rising in you if I started to talk about the use of incense? Some Christians who favor contemporary church services today may associate incense with more traditional or ritualistic church practices. In some readers' minds this word may trigger thoughts of the hippies of the late 1960's whose lifestyle was surrounded with flowers, beads, free love, and pot-smoking. Other people may associate incense with some yoga master chanting to a foreign goddess. Others may think of a crystal-ball reader hiding in a mystical, gloomy atmosphere. Because of all sorts of previous associations, people very easily base their judgment on "it sounds like," rather than on what the Bible teaches.

Most Christians make this mistake simply because related concepts never have been explained from a biblical and practical perspective. If they had an association to truth, then they would be able to understand and make accurate judgments.

Incense, for example, is mentioned over 100 times in the Bible. It was under God's specific instructions that the Jews used incense in their worship. Among other functions, it was counted as a symbol of men's praise and worship rising unto God. In the New Testament, we read about the wise men bringing frankincense and myrrh to honor the young child Jesus (Matt. 2:11).

We understand from the practical perspective that the sense of smell is one of the most powerful avenues affecting people's thought patterns. For example, when you drive your car past a bakery, the smell in the air can make you forget your present course and cause you to dream for a moment about the joy of eating a hot cinnamon roll. You might even salivate. Similarly, walking into a home filled with the aroma of freshly baked apple pie can trigger pleasurable thoughts from years ago.

So, too, incense is known to focus people's thoughts. A fragrance in the air can create an atmosphere separate from the harsh, busy world and cause people to forget their problems, the same way that music does. It is an effective tool in helping men turn their minds and hearts from the world so they may seek God with their whole soul.

Now please do not take me wrong. I am not

trying to get you to use incense. I simply am trying to help you see how previous associations can cause you to reject things wrongly. If you always have associated incense with evil occult practices or ritualistic, religious ceremonies, then you will be reluctant to learn how God intended it to be used. So long as you judge on the basis of associations, you likely will be blind to spiritual truths.

Some Christians who have had past experience in various occult practices tend to be blinded concerning many spiritual realities. These are the people who became Christians, but in order to overcome their evil involvements of the past, they went to the opposite extreme and denied all spiritual reality, even warning others to stay away. This over-defensiveness is the natural response when a person has put his trust in something at one time and then later discovered it to be false. They feel deceived, robbed, cheated— and, indeed, they may have been. However, the hurt they bear causes them to be over-sensitive and even deceived again in their own perception. This is especially true with regard to Christians who once were involved in occult practices.

Compare this over-defensiveness with Jim, a man I met a few years ago who had gone through a painful divorce. When I met him, he was scared of anything involving commitment. So hurt was he from his past that he considered all commitments his enemy. For example, he was renting a small building for his business, and when the owner came to ask him to sign a year-long lease, he exploded in anger. When I asked him why, he justified himself by saying that his past had taught him to stay away from commitments. What he really learned from his past was distorted, and it gave him a twisted perspective of life, which hindered all his endeavors for years to come.

I have been guilty myself of over-reacting because of past pain. I was raised in a very traditional church. I put my faith in that church. When I was a young adult, someone taught me some Bible truths that my own church never had discussed. Consequently, I felt that I had been deceived into believing only half the truth. In reaction, I went to the extreme of hating that particular denomination, and I warned people to stay away. My arguments against them were very convincing, and I used various Bible verses to show why that church was wrong. I never realized back then that I was speaking out of hurt. Today, over twenty years later, I can look back more objectively and see that I had been taught many truths, and I am grateful that I was raised in a godly home. It is true that certain biblical truths were neglected in my childhood church, but many things they accomplished for me definitely were of God.

Now, see how defensiveness has blinded some people who were involved in occult practices before becoming Christians. Picture Joe for example. Joe is a Christian today who was deeply involved in the New Age Movement before turning his life over to Jesus Christ. He put all his faith in those teachers. He thought they offered the answers to life's problems. When he received Jesus into his life, he had to renounce all involvement with spiritual practices in which he formerly engaged. That time of his life was a great battle for him. Today he feels cheated. His teachers lied to him. No wonder he spends much time today warning Christians to stay away from anything sounding mystical. His intentions are good, and Christians need to be warned about the dangers involved with various occult activities. However, Joe's perception is twisted negatively by his own hurt.

A tragedy facing the Body of Christ today is that people who do a large percentage of our teaching on spiritual subjects are the witch-hunters and Christians who have come out of evil practices. Our Christian bookstores stock many books written by people who have defensive postures, rather than offensive. This has created an unjust fear in the minds of many Christians. Therefore, it is difficult to use spiritual terminology. It is easy to be misunderstood. Christians have been trained to associate spiritual concepts with evil practices, rather than search the Bible for themselves to discover truth.

We, the Church, never will overcome evil by fear and defensiveness. Surely, there will be an increase of false prophets in the last days, but God's people must overcome. It is time to set aside fears and get into God's provisions for our lives. The world around us never will be won to Jesus by a negative campaign. They must be given God's answers for the hunger they have within them to know spiritual reality. Our greatest defense against evil is not an unlimited number of warnings, but rather the truth of God's power and a biblical understanding of the spiritual realm.

Please, do let yourself be deceived into judging on the basis of "it sounds like." As we taught in Volume I, the true basis for our discernment must be:

1. agreement with the written Word of God,
2. fruit produced over the long term, and
3. the exaltation of Jesus Christ.

With accurate discernment, let's continue.

The Emanating Spirit

The spiritual presence of a person extends not only over other people, but also over things, events, and circumstances. When a homeowner accepts responsibility for his home, he covers that home spiritually. The teenager who claims his bedroom as his own will leave his spiritual impression upon that room. The artist who paints a picture imparts his own spirit into his painting. A person who takes great care and interest in organizing a large event which involves thousands of people actually will be extending his spirit over the entire event.

Anything for which a person takes responsibility and, in a sense, claims as his own, will bear the spiritual imprint of that person.

Therefore, wherever a person places his foot with authority, he deposits a measure of his own spiritual energy. As Abraham walked through the Promised Land, knowing in his heart that it was to belong to his descendants, he literally was planting spiritual seeds and taking possession of it. As the Jews walked around Jericho they were claiming the city as theirs.

When a person buys a piece of land or a new home, he inhabits it not only physically (and legally), but spiritually, as well. Often the very act of giving money to purchase something releases one's own spirit to cover the object. Money that has been earned with personal sacrifice becomes an extension of that person's spirit. On the other hand, when some possession is obtained through thievery or is unearned as a gift, it rarely is possessed spiritually, and, hence, will be lost in time. Whenever money is invested with thought and care, it carries with it some of the authority of the person.

A person's signature also carries the mark of his spirit. When a person signs his name with authority, he is revealing his heart in some way. Depending upon what he is signing, in various degrees he will be giving his commitment or making his thoughts known. When a person signs a historical document, such as a founding constitution of a country, which may be at the risk of his own life, that act may extend his authority for years or generations into the future. Every time a person signs his name with authority, he is leaving a deposit of himself upon that which the signature represents.

Spoken words are also avenues through which people may release spiritual energy. There is a literal substance and force behind spoken words. The significance of spoken words is so important that we will discuss it in Chapter 6, and there examine Bible verses which address the spiritual nature of the spoken word.

Even our thoughts may release spiritual forces which influence the things around us. This concept, too, is so significant that we will take a later chapter to explain it in more detail.

What is important for us to identify at this point is how spiritual substance is released from an individual's heart whenever they accept personal responsibility associated with their own possessions, works of creativity, labors, money, signature, words, or thoughts.

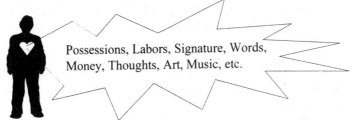

Possessions, Labors, Signature, Words, Money, Thoughts, Art, Music, etc.

As you think of spiritual forces being released from an individual, it is helpful to make several comparisons with natural light. We know that light functions according to natural laws, but several Bible passages draw comparisons between light and the spirit of a man. Similarly, we can make a few comparisons that help us understand some of the ways in which the spirit of a man emanates out from his innermost being.

As light projects out from a source, so also do the rivers of life flow forth. Light can travel far from its source, and so can the spiritual energy within a person emanate far beyond the physical body.

A scientific fact that we know about natural light is that it consists of many different colors. If we take a glass prism and allow sunlight to pass through it, the light going in will be divided into all the colors of the rainbow. There are even some colors which human eyes cannot see.

Add to this fact another truth which scientists have learned as they study light: Different colors of light have differing qualities of penetration. It is because of these differing penetrations that water plants of various colors grow at different levels in the ocean. For example, green algae grow close to the surface of the ocean, while red algae grow at greater depths. The red algae can grow at those greater depths because the light which they absorb penetrates deeper into the water. Different colors of light penetrate in different ways.

These scientific facts can be used to illustrate the outflowing of the human spirit. Some spiritual energy seems to flow within the person flooding the soul, quickening the thought processes and other inner elements. Life energy also fills the physical body, making it alive and able to function. Another form of spirit energy reaches beyond the individual, influencing his countenance or even encompassing his body, thus creating a unique presence. As we have been explaining, the human spirit also extends far beyond the physical location of the person, influencing things, circumstances, and other people.

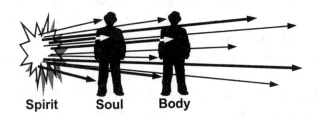

Spirit   **Soul**   **Body**

It is important to note before we go on that the various flows of spiritual energy from within can act separately from one another. For example, the flow which produces a bright countenance upon a person may be very strong; at the same time the energy enveloping the rest of his body can be weak. One person may have a very strong presence about him, and yet not have a spirit which emanates far beyond that. Another may not have enough spiritual life within to keep his body healthy, but he may have spiritual energy extending to a far distant place. These varying flows will become evident as we continue.

Let's conclude this chapter with a story of some native people who live in a primitive region of the world. They were on a long journey by foot and after several hours of walking they sat down for a rest. When asked by a foreigner why they were stopping, they responded, "To let our souls catch up with our bodies."

Before embracing or rejecting this explanation, it is worth giving some credit to the wisdom of such peoples. Often, we who live in modern, developed countries of the world look down on

primitive peoples, assuming that they are igno-
rant and foolish. Having traveled to several
third-world countries myself, I often have been
surprised by their intelligence. For example, it is
common in remote regions of the world to find
people fluent in several languages. Though they
may not be able to read, they have deep, wise
thinkers among them. In fact, most have spent
far more time during their life contemplating the
meaning, purpose, and values of life than the
average city-dweller. Sitting under the stars,
gathered around a fire, or resting under a ba-
nana tree, they talk to one another concerning
the issues of life. Furthermore, they have a freedom of thought which is not seen among those
who have been trained with a Western frame-
work.

If we were to look at the primitive hikers'
words, "To let our souls catch up with our bodies," we would err in trying to bring them into a
Western understanding. However, as Christians
we can fit them into our biblical standard of
truth. Perhaps it would be better to say, "To let
our souls be restored as our spiritual energy
returns and mounts within us." Of course, we
also can explain that they were waiting for their
physical bodies to rest, and that would be a valid
explanation. However, our whole view of man
allows us to see that the entire man—body, soul
and spirit—is involved even in common activity
such as walking.

Spiritual Forces
In the Natural World

The spirit of a person carries with it the personality, strength, faith, love, etc., of that individual. To the degree that the Christian is joined in heart to God, his spirit is one with the Holy Spirit, and, hence, the energy of the Holy Spirit also flows out to those people or things which are touched. The devil also can add his influence to the spiritual flow of a person (Volume III, Chapter 6). At this point, we will not spend much time distinguishing good from bad; rather we will show the principle that *whatever is in a person, good or bad, it flows out to influence people, objects, circumstances, and events.*

All people are subject, to some degree, to the spiritual influences given off by others. At a sports event where everyone is excited, the newcomer easily is enveloped by the atmosphere. When a salesman is full of energy to sell, he may change your attitude toward his product. When someone is very angry, the energy in the air may set others on edge. At a funeral, where many people are mourning, there will be pressure upon even the unknown visitor to be sorrowful.

The spiritual forces are most powerful when coming from people bonded together. For example two close friends can be a tremendous influence upon each other. A husband or wife may be sensitive to every feeling of his or her spouse. When all the people with whom you work have good thoughts toward you, you will find more spiritual energy available to you.

These spiritual forces are especially strong when coming forth from a person of authority, and, in particular, if the position of authority relates directly to the recipient's life. A father has great spiritual influence over his son. A mother's care releases powerful blessings for her children. A grandmother, through her prayers, can bless the children and grandchildren whose photos she keeps on her mantle. A political leader can impart spiritual influences into those over whom he has been given authority. Similarly, the boss at a business can release spiritual energy into his employees by the attitude he has toward them.

All people can influence each other positively or negatively, but authority has an advantage because spiritual dynamics work accordingly.

We can see an extreme example of this by reading First Corinthians 5:1-5. In that passage, we read how the Apostle Paul dealt with a problem in the early Church. A certain man was committing immoral acts, and the local congregation would not deal with it, so Paul used his authority spiritually. He wrote:

> For I, on my part, though absent in body but present in spirit, have already judged him who has so committed this, as though I were present. In the name of our Lord Jesus, when you are assembled, and I with you in spirit, with the power of our Lord Jesus, I have decided to deliver such a one to Satan for the destruction of his flesh, that his spirit may be saved in the day of the Lord Jesus (I Cor. 5:3-5).

Many truths can be learned from these verses, but let me give a caution first.

By quoting this passage, we are not giving credence to people releasing curses or evil onto other people. We point out that Paul was exercising this authority in the name of Jesus, with His power, and therefore, in God's will. Recognizing that, we also must realize that Paul had authority from God in this church. He was their "father in the faith," having labored over them for years. He also had apostolic oversight of these people. Acknowledging that relationship, we can see the authority God had given Paul.

He used that authority. He said, "...being absent in body, but present in spirit...I have decided to deliver such a one to Satan...." Those words are sobering.

41

Although we never may see authority being used as severely as in First Corinthians 5, authority does exist. *In the realm of the spirit, authority is a very exacting, governing force.* When a certain soldier came to Jesus, he said:

> "Lord,...just say the word, and my servant will be healed. For I, too, am a man under authority, with soldiers under me; and I say to this one, 'Go!' and he goes, and to another, 'Come!' and he comes, and to my slave, 'Do this!' and he does it" (Matt. 8:8b-9).

Authority is arranged in an ascending/descending pattern. Just as water runs downhill in the natural world, good and bad most easily run down the chain of command in the spiritual world.

When speaking of love, strength, or other blessings flowing from one individual to another, we should understand that some openness of heart is necessary on the part of the recipient. The Apostle Paul wrote to the Colossians that he was "with them in spirit." This was stated in part to encourage them, so they would take strength from his love and concern. Similarly, children can draw upon the spiritual attributes of their parents, but their hearts must be open to receive. On the other hand, people may reject the spiritual influence of others by the opposition within their own hearts toward those people.

Let's turn our attention from people being influenced and see how spiritual energy can change things, events, and circumstances. It does not matter whether that energy is released through spoken words, thoughts, or the mere projection of a person's spirit. All things in this natural world are subject to energy from the spiritual world.

An obvious example is from the truth Jesus gave us about a mountain being moved when it is addressed in faith (Mark 12:23). The mountain itself responds.

When God spoke, the world itself came into existence. Of course, God's faith was perfect and He has all authority, but we need to recognize the principle here. When faith releases that which is spiritual into the natural, the natural must respond, yield, and change.

When spiritual energy flows out of a man, it influences the natural world in accordance to what is within his heart. Whatever it is that the person believes, that very thing is projected wherever his spirit goes. The ideas, desires, and goals of the individual influence the world accordingly. The greater the faith of the person, the greater will be his spiritual influence upon the natural world.

Even objects are affected.

To understand this, we must recognize that when spiritual energy is released, it actually goes *into* the things toward which it is projected. As we mentioned earlier, the artist deposits a measure of his spirit in his work. The homeowner leaves his spiritual energy upon his home. Spiritual impressions are left upon everything which has contact with a person's spirit.

This concept—that things can hold spiritual energy—is critical. We read in the Book of Acts how handkerchiefs of Paul were carried to the sick and many were healed (Acts 19:12). The Jewish priests were not permitted to wear their clothing both in the presence of the Lord and in the midst of the people, lest they "transmit holiness to the people with their garments" (Ezek. 44:19). In II Kings 13:21, we are told the story of a dead man being thrown into Elisha's grave, and there was still enough power in Elisha's bones to raise the dead man to life. Several Bible passages talk about certain portions of land being holy, while others have been desecrated.

First Timothy 4:4 tells us that all created things respond to spiritual input:

> For everything created...is sanctified by the means of the word of God and prayer.

Here we clearly are told that prayer and speaking the Word of God over things "sanctifies," that is, makes them holy.

Yes, sanctuaries where people worship God do become holy. The people of God in the Old Testament often built altars to God, and those locations became holy ground. Of course, God is spirit and our worship never should be restricted to a certain location (John 4:20-24), but there is also a reality to holiness literally being transmitted to natural things.

Furthermore, we are beginning to see how the "spiritual value" of things can change. Spiritual energy literally is deposited into natural things.

On the negative side, we can talk about the evil release of power through things. For example, one of the most common practices of witchcraft is to project spiritual energy through what is known as a "power object" or a "familiar object." A witch may take a small object and secretly plant it at a location near the people whom she wants to influence. Then as the witch meditates upon that object and claims it her possession, she may begin emitting from that object her own spiritual influence into the surroundings.

Some naturally-minded Christians today mock the idea that evil people can exercise any spiritual power. The Bible itself is very clear that such evil exercises are real, and we are warned not to be involved (Deut. 18:10-12). The fact that the Bible tells us not to be involved implies that such things are real—evil, but real.

The list of examples of related present-day experiences could be extensive, but here I will mention just one. A few years ago a minister friend of mine was having great success in his church. People were being saved and great blessings were evident in his work. Then a woman in the congregation made a doily to be placed upon the pulpit in the sanctuary. She began making other items also and placing them around the building. It was not until later that the leaders came to understand the controlling forces within this woman's life. Shortly after she began "decorating" the church, the minister discovered tremendous forces against him as he tried to speak. It was as if a wall had been erected against him. It was only a short time before a multitude of problems erupted and the church collapsed.

Of course, we do not want to blame all church problems on witchcraft. I do not believe that the enemy can overcome Christians unless those Christians have opened the door in some fashion to evil. However, we do want to point out the reality of evil curses. There are witches and evil men at work in the world. One of their common practices is to place power objects within a place where God seems to be blessing, and then they exert evil powers by claiming that location as their possession and, hence, releasing evil forces.

We can learn from this that Christians should claim that which God has given to them. To give up responsibility is to release it to the enemy. To hold it is to take spiritual authority over it.

It is important to note that the battle between good and evil is in no way a "fair war." What Christians need to realize is that, as they tap into God's power, they are releasing the kingdom which is already victorious over Satan. Sometimes people misunderstand this and picture two opposing powers facing each other in some type of "star wars encounter." In reality, the battle between good and evil is not one of good and bad people shooting bolts of light toward each other. No. The proper perspective is more of a victorious kingdom being released through the Christian, and whenever it is released, victory is inevitable. Light overcomes and expels darkness. All that is required for the Christian to win is to act according to God's will. When we release His will, we release His power.

It is not only this good and evil struggle that we want to address. There is also a reality to the simple power of faith. When a person holds responsibility for something, whether that person is a Christian or not, his spiritual energy projects forth and influences those things: "Be it done to you according to your faith." Whatever is locked within the heart of the individual, spiritual energy will emanate to influence things accordingly.

It is the author's belief that an automobile for which its owner has taken responsibility will run better. The homeowner who cares for his home in some way will release spiritual energy to make the paint last longer, the wood to not rot as quickly, and the heating system to function better. Of course, if a person has little faith and they believe that their own possessions will fall apart, then they release negative forces. Spiritual energy actually and literally flows out to bring things into alignment with the faith of the person whose spirit permeates them. The Bible even tells us that if a person has enough faith, they can drink deadly poison and it will not hurt them (Mark 16:18). We are not encouraging people to drink poison nor to test God. However, we are teaching the principle that whether a person believes positively or negatively, that for which they bear spiritual responsibility is influenced.

In Chapter 7 we will teach concerning when the release of spiritual power is according to God's will. Please, do not at this point assume that we are teaching any unbiblical extremes. We simply hope to point out the reality of this release of spiritual power. Later, we will explain the appropriate use of it.

Just as objects and possessions may be influenced, so also are circumstances and events. People with a strong flow of spiritual energy find their paths being supernaturally established ahead of them. For reasons that cannot be explained naturally, a person with great authority will seem to meet the right person at the right time, be in the right place just when they are needed, have closed doors open before them, and find key opportunities appearing at just the right moment.

We can explain this phenomenon as the hand of God moving on behalf of a person. Indeed, we know that "the steps of a man are established by the Lord" (Ps. 37:23a). However, we want you to see this in association with the spiritual power flowing out from a person's innermost being. Of course, God helps His children, and He does reach down sovereignly from heaven and make a way where there is no way. But we also must recognize that His power flows through people. So do both the human spirit and evil spirits have power. There is a literal force which emanates from people in accordance with their authority and faith, which acts upon objects, events, and circumstances.

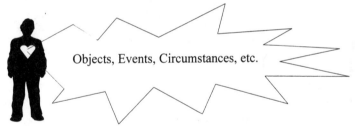

Objects, Events, Circumstances, etc.

Let me say it again. We, as Bible-believing Christians, understand that the natural world does not function independently of the spiritual world. Christians, more than any other people, should understand this truth. The natural world was created out of the spiritual world. We believe in the spiritual realm. We, as Bible-believers, do not see ourselves as mere natural creatures. We are humans existing in both the spiritual world and the natural world, simultaneously. We have, through faith, the authority to draw spiritual substance from the spiritual world and release it into this natural realm. This is the biblical concept of how the spiritual and the natural worlds influence each other.

6

The Power of the Spoken Word

Spiritual energy is released with the spoken word. Let's see how this works.

First consider God. When He spoke into existence this natural world, we recognize creative power within His words (e.g., Gen. 1:3). Hebrews 11:3 tells us that the entire world was brought into existence as God spoke.

Jesus testified to the spiritual nature of His own words when He said to His disciples, "The words that I have spoken to you are spirit and are life" (John 6:63b). Notice that the words themselves "are spirit." In another passage our Lord declared, "Heaven and earth will pass away, but My words shall not pass away" (Matt. 24:32). Here we learn of the enduring—even eternal—quality of His words.

When we talk about the words spoken by common men, we do not want to assume or imply that men have the same power within their words that God does. However, we are identifying a biblical principle here. Words consist of more than sound vibrations moving through the atmosphere. Our words may not be as forceful as God's, but to some degree, they, too, carry spiritual substance with them.

The Bible explains to us that the power behind words is based on faith in the person's heart. Jesus said:

> "Truly I say to you, whoever says to this mountain, 'Be taken up and cast into the sea,' and does not doubt in his heart, but believes that what he says is going to happen, it shall be granted him" (Mark 11:23).

We have pointed out how that the heart is the seat of faith (Rom. 10:10) and from it "flow the issues of life" (Prov. 4:23). The greater a person's faith—that is, his confidence in what he speaks—the greater will be the spiritual force behind those words.

Paul exhorted every Christian to exercise his gifts according to the grace given to him, "...if prophecy, according to the proportion of his faith" (Rom. 12:6). Here we see again the role faith plays as a person speaks out. According to one's faith, the spiritual power flows out with the spoken word.

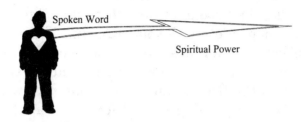

Spoken Word

Spiritual Power

The reality that words contain spiritual substance can be seen in the following example from my own life, to which I trust you will be able to relate. As I travel and speak at many churches and Christian conferences, I notice that different groups of people receive my messages with various degrees of openness. One time I was teaching on a subject that was difficult for my audience to embrace at the time. After leaving that group, I noticed a warfare going on in my mind. For about twenty-four hours after the conference ended, I continually was reviewing and defending to myself the things I had spoken. Thoughts were whirring through my mind so fast and furiously that I could not sleep that night. I had experienced this type of turmoil before, but I never had related it to the willingness of people to receive my message. I decided to start observing in the future how and when I had to go through such mind battles to determine if, indeed, there was an association between the two.

Sure enough, as the years have gone by, I have observed that the mind battles are most intense following meetings at which I have spoken "hard-to-receive messages." It was as if the words I had spoken were *returning to me.*

Then one day I was traveling home after a difficult conference. My mind would not rest. Finally, when I arrived home I could not sleep, so I paced the floor of our living room, reviewing my words and praying to God for peace. After some time passed, I remembered what God said about His Words not returning void (Isaiah 55:11— KJV). I sensed that God wanted me to take on this same stance of authority, so I stood in the middle of the room, and with all the spiritual force and faith in my heart I declared, "My words shall not return void!" I pushed the words out of my system and back to the people to whom I had spoken them. As soon as I had done this, peace came and I was able to rest.

What I have concluded is that words which are not received by the people to whom they are spoken, may return to the source individual. It is not the sound waves in the air which return, but the spiritual substance of those words. That person then makes a decision whether to defend those words or to receive them back. If he receives them back, they become void, of no effect, and the people who heard them forget or somehow ignore the message. If, on the other hand, the speaker does not shrink back from that which he has spoken, the substance of those words remains out there accomplishing what they have been sent out to do, according to the faith behind them.

Once I understood these principles, I discovered how easy it is to increase the authority of what I say. After a meeting I determine in my heart that I will not shrink back from believing the things I have taught. Also, I find amazing strength in the support of someone I trust. For example, if my wife, or a friend who sometimes travels with me, makes a reassuring comment to me after a meeting, such as, "You did good," I find an agreement that gives me strength. That agreement is not as powerful if it comes from someone who might be just trying to encourage me, but when it comes from someone who I know will be honest with me, I find that their simple reaffirming words can enable me to stand free from all "rebounding" words. More important, it seems to add authority to what I have said, making my words stay out there accomplishing what I have sent them out to do.

Comprehending these principles shines light on why Jesus instructed His disciples to brush the dust off their feet if people did not accept their message (Matt. 10:14). That act would be an act of establishing what they had said. It not only would protect them from spiritual bombardment, but also would keep their words from being erased in the minds of those who heard.

I use the terminology, "spiritual bombardment." This is what actually is happening. As the hearers reject the things spoken to them, the words go back to the speaker. It is not always a conscious rejection, but more a realignment of their own thoughts so that there is no resting place for the new ideas which were presented to them. Those dislodged words then return to the originator. The bombardment consists of spiritual substance, yet sometimes it may be physically felt, especially upon the forehead or face of the person, leaving them feeling as if they were beat up. For this reason God made the prophet's "face like flint" when he had to deliver a strong message to stubborn people (Ezek. 3:9).

Not all words carry the same weight or authority. When spoken by a person, the spiritual force is determined by that individual's faith, intensity of conviction, passion, agreement with others, and depth of decision. Some people carry more authority simply because of who they are. For this reason, when people with great authority speak, it impacts many lives. Another person could verbalize the same things and very few, if any, people would be influenced.

The greater the time and sacrifice invested in the formulation of a thought, the greater will be the force behind it. Usually, there is more authority in the written word than in everyday conversation because the writer has taken more time to think through exactly what he desires to say.

Some words carry authority that compels others to repeat them. For example, a certain speaker with much authority may speak a profound truth to one or two people. In such cases, it is as if that truth cannot be contained within just their spirits. The listeners will be compelled, therefore, to repeat it again and again until the substance of those words has been distributed to however many people it takes to contain the related authority.

Not just *truth* contains authority, but all words have some level of substance to them. Enough thought may be put into a new idea, story, or even a joke so that it bears repeating and sharing with others. Sometimes in telling a joke, people feel as if there were a little bit more "juice" in it, and so it may be told one more time. Eventually, however, the substance wears out and no one else will hear or receive it, unless someone adds their own spiritual substance in telling the story. People experience these forces in their daily lives all the time, but they rarely identify from whence they come.

The more personal responsibility people accept for their own words, the more authority that accompanies them. When a person accepts responsibility in his heart for many lives or for the distant future, the spiritual substance within his words increases in a corresponding fashion.

Words or messages also have authority even when they did not originate with the speaker, but rather were taken from the beliefs of a larger group of people. As the spiritual substance is drawn within a person, he may pass it on and, hence, transmit the authority of others.

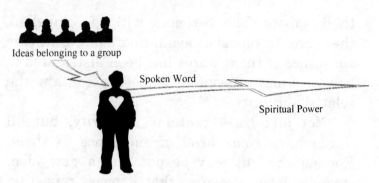

Ideas belonging to a group

Spoken Word

Spiritual Power

Communication between two people is both a spiritual and a natural process. We are aware of the sound waves which carry our words from one to another, but we also must identify the spiritual transmission that takes place. We dare say that the spiritual transmission is more important than the natural. In many cases, people communicate without actually speaking vocally. It is common for people who are bonded together in spirit to know to some degree what the other is thinking. Of course, effective communication requires that sound waves actually travel from one individual to the ears of another, but there also must be a transmission of spiritual energy.

Since words carry spiritual substance, people must receive that substance if they are to truly hear and be changed by those words. Unless there is some kind of open door in the spirit between two people, they will be unable to communicate effectively. This open door can be either through a spiritual bonding between the two individuals, or it can be through the yielding of one person's spirit to receive from the other.

The Apostle John wrote in his first letter about one area in which a spiritual union must exist between two people before they can communicate. He wrote:

> We are from God; he who knows God listens to us; he who is not from God does not listen to us (I John 4:6a).

Jesus stated this same principle to the Pharisees, saying:

> "He who is of God hears the words of God; for this reason you do not hear them, because you are not of God" (John 8:47).

In these passages we see how people's spiritual condition determines whether or not they will be able to communicate.

These principles are applicable whether or not a person is a Christian. The depth of spiritual union between two people determines their ability to communicate. Any two people can talk about superficial things, but the deeper the content, the deeper the spiritual interaction involved. When two people's hearts are directed in two different directions, they will have a difficult time communicating.

The experienced preacher realizes that before he can communicate effectively, he must have the people's hearts all oriented the same as his. The anointing of God upon a minister's life does this very thing. It causes the spirits of the listeners to "hear" his words. King David praised God, "Who subdues my people under me" (Ps. 144:2d). We mentioned how there must be either a bonding in spirit or a yielding of the listener to the speaker before there can be effective communication. With the anointing, God causes the people to yield. His presence in some way manifests, and in His presence every one bows in spirit.

As the Spirit of God abides upon a group of people, communication is extremely easy. One person can say something and others will understand it. On Pentecost Day, we even see the disciples speaking in tongues and the people hearing it in their own language. In contrast, when demonic influence and closed hearts are present, two people can sit side-by-side and completely misinterpret what the other is saying.

It is usually easy to determine whether or not another person is receptive to what you are saying. You can sense whether or not their hearts are directed toward you. You even can be standing in a store at the check-out counter and "feel" a person standing next to you who wants to talk to you. On the other hand, you may stand in front of a large group and sense the resistance. Your child, your spouse, your brother, your neighbor, and all people open or close the doors of their heart. Every person is aware of these principles to one degree or another.

Effective communication depends upon spiritual receptivity. When the walls within a person's spirit are up, they will not hear another person's words completely. If two people have their hearts directed in the same place or toward each other, then communication is easy. This is true because communication is above all else a spiritual transference of energy.

It is also true that words have an almost mysterious way of finding people who are bonded to the speaker. By using the word *mysterious* here, I am referring only to the aspects of how words are transferred between people in an unseen, almost mystical sense. However, they are not truly mysterious if we can explain that mystery, which is what we are doing.

When we say that words *find* the people to whom the speaker is bonded, we are referring to the people who are bonded in heart. The speaker has his heart directed toward the people, and the people have their hearts directed toward him. As we already have explained, words are transferred easily when hearts are bonded.

However, now we want to add a whole new dimension to this phenomenon. The hearers do not even have to be present when the speaker speaks to hear his words.

For example, one Sunday morning pastor Bob spoke a powerful message from the depth of his heart to his congregation. Brother Joe loves pastor Bob, but Joe was unable to attend the meeting that morning because he was home sick in bed. Two days later Mary, who was in the meeting, saw Joe, and in a short time she was stirred within to share some of the key points which pastor Bob spoke. Even though Joe was not present, the words his pastor spoke eventually reached his ears.

This phenomenon is seen in even more "mysterious" ways.

For example, Carol was a missionary to India for 20 years before she returned home. She loved the people of India and those people loved her deeply. She was not going back to the mission field again but occasionally shared in churches about her experiences during those years. One day she was speaking in a certain church, and the Holy Spirit came upon her very powerfully to share her love for those people with whom she had labored. Sitting in the congregation was a young boy who eventually grew up and went to the very same mission field. Something seemed to impact his spirit that day, and he eventually carried the words of Carol back to the same people.

It is our belief that words can travel even beyond the limits we have mentioned thus far. For example, a certain preacher may be standing before a congregation of a hundred people, but his heart is extending toward thousands or toward the entire nation in which he lives. Because of that, his words will have more force behind them than that which can be contained by those people present. All or many of them may be compelled to go out and share with others. Someone eventually may get on the radio and pass on some of that spiritual substance. The message may come across in a different form, perhaps even years later, but it will come forth. The number of people who hear is not determined by the number immediately present as the speaker opens his mouth, but by the number of people he loves and by the extent of his spiritual authority.

Picture this force when we talk about the words of our Lord. He said, "My sheep hear My voice." His sheep are those whose hearts are pointed toward Him. Recognizing the spiritual implications of this, we can see how the words of our Lord find people in whatever country or whatever generation they live. Having perfect faith, Jesus even had the audacity to declare that His words would never pass away.

We also can talk about negative words reaching certain people. For example, Bill was gossiping about John. About three days later, the words Bill spoke were reported back to John. They were not the exact words, because gossip often changes as it is passed from one person to another. However, the *negative substance* of the gossip was carried until it reached back to John.

Ecclesiastes 10:20 teaches us that negative words spoken in secret will fly like a bird to the ears of kings, leaders, and wealthy people. Notice the association with authority that words follow.

When something negative is said about a person of authority, those words tend to reach his ears sooner or later.

Yes, words carry spiritual substance with them. That substance dissipates according to the faith behind those words. The greater the authority, heart conviction, and responsibility accepted by the speaker, the more enduring will be the substance of those words.

7

Spiritual Energy— When is it Right?

Every human being uses the spiritual abilities we have been discussing, whether or not he realizes it. Even Christians who think only in terms of natural forces have a spirit which extends beyond their physical bodies. Every human being releases, to some degree, spiritual substance with their words. Every human being exerts unseen forces upon the people and things around him. All of us were created with a spirit, and that spirit has influence upon both the spiritual and natural worlds 24 hours each day.

It is essential at this point that we begin including in our discussion the appropriate use of these spiritual abilities. When should a Christian apply these principles by a conscious act of his own will? We are especially interested in man's taking the initiative in these things. What can we initiate ourselves, and what should we wait for God to sovereignly inspire us to do?

To answer these questions we must introduce another biblical concept. In several places in the original Greek Bible the word "*metron*" is used. In English it usually is translated "measure." We are told in Romans 12:3 that to every man is given a *measure*, or a *metron*, of faith. In Second Corinthians 10:13, Paul wrote:

> But we will not boast beyond our measure, but within the measure of the sphere which God apportioned to us as a measure, to reach even as far as you.

Paul explained that he would not go beyond his own God-given sphere of influence or beyond his own metron. In passages like these, this word refers to *the level of faith and the spiritual authority which God has given a person.*

Each person, Christian or non-Christian, has a specific metron. It includes everything over which a person has responsibility. A parent's metron includes his/her children. A businessman's metron is over his business. A police officer has a metron which includes the responsibilities given to him. A homeowner has God-given authority to do what he wants with his home. A teacher has a metron over the classroom of which he is in charge. All authority comes from God, and whether that authority is over natural or spiritual things, one's metron encompasses it.

Metron (God-given responsibilities): Children, possessions, job, etc.

Jesus has an unlimited metron. His authority covers everything (Matt. 28:18). He is the Alpha and Omega (Rev. 1:17). John 3:34-35 tells us that He has the Spirit without measure, that is, without limits to His metron. There are no boundaries to His metron and the Spirit flows out of Him to whatever extent He chooses.

We, however, have limits to our metron. *Our authority is related to what God presently has entrusted to us.* Paul wrote that for his own life he would not go beyond his sphere of influence (II Cor. 10:13). He knew the limits of his God-given authority. We as Christians have authority in both the natural and the spiritual realms, but we must understand the limits of our own metron.

Some Christians may have a difficult time understanding this "limited authority," because the emphasis in their teaching has been that we, as believers, can do "all" things through Christ Jesus, and that we have been seated with our Lord in heavenly places far above all rule and authority. Their theology dictates a belief that Christians already have all authority.

It is true that we have all things in Christ, but there is also a reality to our growing into them. God deals with us as His children. As we prove faithful, He releases to us that which He has promised.

This relationship between the authority promised to us and the authority we actually experience is parallel to how the Hebrew people took the Promised Land. It all was given to them by God. The land was theirs by promise. However, after they crossed the Jordan River and entered the land of promise, they could not possess it when or how they chose. God instructed them to take the cities in the specific order He would indicate to them. God also warned them that if they attempted to take cities which He was not leading them into, they would be defeated (Ex. 23:20-30; Deut. 7:22). Even though the whole land was theirs by promise, they only could occupy it as they obeyed God and progressively filled what they already had taken. In similar fashion, the fullness of God's power and authority has been promised to the believer. However, our experience of it is progressive as we step out, faithfully doing what God leads each step of the way.

Jesus said, "For whoever has, to him shall more be given" (Mark 4:25a). "To have" something in this sense is to possess it spiritually. When we accept the responsibilities which God already has given to us, then God increases our authority. In terms of our metron, as we fulfill our present responsibilities, our metron increases.

Within a person's present metron, that individual has authority. This means that a person has the right to do what he desires to do. We are not saying that you can do whatever you want and get away with it. No. God will hold you accountable for everything you do. What we want to understand here is that you have the "right" to do what you want to do within your metron because God has given you the authority to do it. Of course, you should endeavor to accomplish the will of God within all that He has assigned to you. But we hope you see that God gives you the authority to work within your metron.

Because you have authority, you can take the initiative. That is what it means to have authority. It is in your hands. You decide. For example, if you are a homeowner, then you have the right to decide what color you want to paint your house. If you have children, God expects you to take the initiative to provide for them and to raise them. It is your job to take whatever initiative is necessary to do what needs to be done within your metron.

In relationship to spiritual things, within the Christian's spirit is the wisdom and the direction to know how to manage his God-given metron. An anointing is given to help a believer manage his metron. First John 2:27 tells us:

> And as for you, the anointing which you received from Him abides in you, and you

have no need for anyone to teach you; but as His anointing teaches you about all things, and is true and is not a lie, and just as it has taught you, you abide in Him.

The believer has within himself the "knowing" concerning how and when he is suppose to act within his God-given authority. God's understanding already has been deposited there. The anointing "teaches" him. It supernaturally guides him concerning the when and how of his actions.

In the area of one's anointing, the Christian does not need God to visit him supernaturally to tell him what to do every step of the way. No. God already has given him the wisdom. It resides within him. Just as a child matures and no longer needs his parents to tell him what clothes to wear, so also a believer should not expect God to speak to him supernaturally and to tell him what to do when the anointing already is directing him. *The Christian is wrong in waiting around for God's additional external direction when he already has the internal anointing guiding him in the area of his metron.*

To understand these principles, look at some biblical examples. In the life of the priest Eli, we can see how God expected him to take the initiative to exercise his own authority. Eli's metron included both his sons and the temple worship.

Those were his God-given responsibilities but he failed, and his own sons began committing evil acts in the temple (I Sam. 2:12-17). We are told that Eli sinned by not stopping his sons (I Sam. 3:13). God did not have to come down sovereignly upon Eli and motivate him to fulfill his responsibilities. No. It was Eli's job to motivate himself. He was supposed to take the initiative, because God already had delegated the authority to him.

Examine the life of Moses. It was in his heart to set the Hebrew people free from their captivity; however, as a young man he was unable to do so and he left Egypt defeated, running from Pharaoh. At that point in his life, he had no God-given authority to set the Hebrews free. Later in his life, he received a call from God to return to Egypt and deliver them. Then God gave Moses the authority, and we see Moses having power to release amazing signs and wonders.

An interesting event occurred as Moses led the Hebrews out of Egypt to the edge of the Red Sea. It was there that we see Moses desperately crying out to God to help them. God's response to Moses in that situation is eye-opening. He said:

> "Why are you crying out to
> Me? Tell the sons of Israel to
> go forward" (Ex. 14:15b).

God rebuked Moses. Why? Because Moses already had the authority to bring the people out of captivity. Moses was waiting for God to do something when God was waiting for Moses to do something. Moses did not need to look to God for the directive to divide the sea. He needed to go forward because it was his responsibility. Even though spiritual power was to be used, Moses needed to take the initiative because God already had commissioned him and given him the related authority.

The time God intervenes supernaturally is when He wants us to go *beyond our present metron.* That is when He speaks and empowers in additional supernatural ways. He has the authority to tell us to do whatever He desires. For us rightfully to go beyond our metron requires that He impart new authority into us. Only then can we effectively accomplish His will. Those steps beyond our present authority must be initiated by God. He has to tell us when to take the related steps. *We do not have the authority to initiate such steps because they are not within our present metron.*

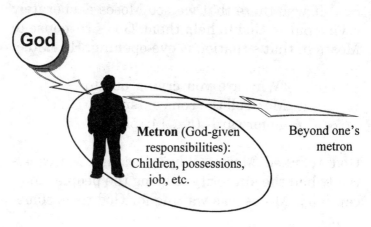

See how this applies to our lives? The first time a certain Christian speaks in tongues, the Holy Spirit must come upon him to impart the ability. Once that person's spirit has been released in this fashion, it is no longer a matter of the Holy Spirit initiating it every time the individual wants to speak out in his new language. The person can do it as he wills. Once the authority has been gained in the spirit to use this gift, it is the responsibility of that individual to continue to exercise it. The individual must take the initiative.

The gift of prophecy works similarly. The first time a Christian is used by God to speak out boldly that which is in his spirit, it is common for him to experience an enlarging of his spirit. While the person is standing in the midst of a congregation, his heart may start beating rapidly, his thoughts begin to race, and he even may feel as if he is going to explode inside. What is that? It is the Holy Spirit energizing his spirit to step out into new areas. Now, we do not want to justify every such experience and say that it is always God, because other things can motivate a person in such a fashion also. What we wish to identify is how God, in such cases, may be taking the initiative and pushing the individual into greater realms of the spirit. Once the related authority has been attained, it is no longer just a matter of God initiating the use of the gift of prophecy. The Christian who has attained a level of authority in this area by an act of his own will can prophesy the will of God within his present metron.

For the same reasons the pastor who has oversight of a flock does not need a visitation from God to tell him everything he must do. No. He already has the anointing within him to do what needs to be done. He has the tools, the wisdom, and the guidance of his own God-given anointing to enable him. Therefore, it is his responsibility to measure up to the level of authority already given.

When we talk about the spirit of a man flowing out, we must understand it in terms of the person's metron. In this respect, Paul said that he would not go beyond his metron (II Cor. 10:13). To the Christians to whom Paul had ministered, he wrote that he was "with them in spirit" (Col. 2:5; I Thes. 2:17; I Cor. 5:3-4). Paul exercised authority over those who were within his metron. However, it would have been wrong for Paul to extend his spiritual influence to a people over whom God had not given him authority.

Similarly, whenever a person today extends his spirit beyond the limits of his God-given authority, he is usurping that authority. He may, whether or not he realizes it, release evil spiritual influences. *God's power only works within God-given authority.* If a person, therefore, extends his spirit to other people wrongly, those people may come under demonic attack. If he releases spiritual substance through his words upon things which are not under his authority, evil energies may be activated. Circumstances, events, and objects all may be influenced, but they only will be affected according to God's will if the person exercising the spiritual authority was given that authority by God.

It is in this fashion that all the gifts, empowerings, and spiritual authorities work. When we are confronted with things requiring more authority than we presently possess, then we need the Holy Spirit to come upon us and impart the additional authority needed. The first time God is moving someone into a new realm, God must initiate it. If He only wants to use that person in that area one time, then He will not impart the ongoing authority. The only time a person may take the initiative to operate in some level of the spirit is if, indeed, God has given him the "abiding authority" and the corresponding anointing which will "abide" within him. Once God has given a person the authority, there will be an inner knowing and an inner guidance system to lead him as to when and how to establish the will of God within his expanded metron. If God has given someone specific authority to accomplish some task, then it is that person's responsibility. Of him who has shall much be required. It is then the individual's responsibility to take the necessary initiative.

As we continue, we will discuss further uses of spiritual power. All of these must be understood in terms of God-given authority. As we discuss sensing things in the spiritual realm, influencing angels and devils, out-of-body experiences, looking into the future, interpreting dreams, etc., we must put them in terms of a person's metron.

It is with this understanding that we can see the fundamental evil involved in witchcraft, occult practices, New Age exercises, astrology, certain experiments in parapsychology, etc. Christians need not deny the reality of these forms of spiritual activities. *What we renounce is the usurping of spiritual authority.* When a witch releases spiritual power upon another person, she is exercising authority which God has not given to her. When a student of transcendental meditation projects his spirit to another place, he is violating spiritual rights. When a man uses extrasensory perception (ESP), to discover information which is outside of his metron, he is opening his spirit up to receive things which are not within his God-given rights. When a medium calls a departed soul back from the dead, he or she is exercising authority which God forbids (Deut. 18:10-11). When the New Agers meditate on worldwide peace and hence try to loose it into this realm, they, indeed, may have well-meaning goals, but unless God initiates such worldwide releasing of energy, it is demonic. Any attempt by any person to go beyond his God-given authority is evil. This hits at the core of Satan's sin itself which is to exalt one's own authority over God.

These principles are vital for the Christian's

life. When the Christian goes beyond his present level of authority, he exposes himself to demonic attack. God warned the Hebrews that they must take the Promised Land only in the timing that He ordained, or the enemies would become too numerous for them and they would be consumed (Ex. 23:20-30). In similar fashion, Christians who step beyond their metrons often experience undue pain and heartache (explained in the next chapter).

It is important for the believer to understand that God gives all authority (Rom. 13:1), and that He alone has the right to expand our metrons when and how He desires. The wise Christian focuses his energies upon managing that which God already has given him. As he proves faithful, God will expand, promote, and exalt him.

Some people, as they read these pages, may be wondering how to apply all the spiritual principles that we have been discussing throughout this book. It is precisely at this point of God-given authority that you must begin. For what has God actually given you responsibility? That is what you must embrace and toward which you must direct your energy toward. Do not try to change the whole world if you have not established the peace of Jesus Christ in your own life. Then work on your home and your relationships. Spend time with your children. Get your finances in order before you try to exert authority over society. Release the presence of God into that which is immediately around you, and let God exalt you

one step at a time. Begin right where you are
presently.

Manipulations
Of the Mind

It is important to identify the relationship between a man's thinking processes and the emanation of his spirit. As a person focuses his heart and thoughts, his spirit may be projected accordingly. That spiritual flow may influence his own being, the natural world around him, and the spiritual world. It is helpful to recognize all three of these areas and how they are influenced.

First, as Christians focus their minds upon the Word of God, they release the blessings of God to some degree into their own lives. Romans 12:2 exhorts us to "be transformed by the renewing of your mind...." The Christian is wise to meditate upon the Word of God continually. As he does, his being may be brought more into alignment with the will of God.

Second, spiritual energy emanates out to conform the natural world to God's will. The Kingdom of God is released as faith in the heart of the believer is at work.

Third, the spiritual world is influenced by our thoughts. Every time a Christian rejects temptation, in some way he is frustrating the plans of Satan. Every time he obeys the biblical mandate to think on that which is pure and holy (Phil. 4:8), he is releasing God's will. Every human being is influencing the spiritual world every day of his life whether or not he realizes it.

At times, people even exert major influence upon spiritual entities. In Second Corinthians 10:3-5, for example, we are told:

> For though we walk in the flesh, we do not war according to the flesh, for the weapons of our warfare are not of the flesh, but divinely powerful for the destruction of fortresses. We are destroying speculations and every lofty thing raised up against the knowledge of God, and we are taking every thought captive to the obedience of Christ.

Notice that as Christians take thoughts captive they are destroying "fortresses." The spiritual world literally is influenced either positively or negatively, contingent upon our thoughts.

In the book of Daniel we can read about a struggle that went on in the spiritual dimension while Daniel fasted and prayed for 21 days (Dan. 10:1-14). As Daniel was praying, the angel was advancing toward Daniel but the "prince of the power of Persia" withstood him. Finally, the angel succeeded and Daniel received the answer he was seeking. There was a real relationship between the activities in which Daniel was engaged through prayer and that which occurred in the spirit world.

It is not only Christians who have this authority to affect the spiritual world. As we have explained, non-Christians also have the power to bind or loose, but not in relation to the Kingdom of God (Vol. I, Chapter 7). In Jude, verse 8, we read about the activity of evil men who challenge spirit beings in the spiritual world:

> Yet in the same manner these men, also by dreaming, defile the flesh, and reject authority, and revile angelic majesties.

Notice the mechanism by which these men do their evil deeds: "by dreaming." Dreaming in this context is not talking about the visions we receive while asleep. It refers here to the manipulation of the thoughts within one's own mind. When a person, Christian or non-Christian, consciously alters the thoughts he has within himself, he at times is exerting authority over the spiritual realm.

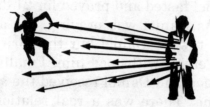

It is this "manipulation of the mind" that we need to examine. When yogis and New Agers talk about meditation, they usually are referring to actively conforming the visions and ideas in their minds to their desired goals. They will set aside time just to sit and think along certain lines. It is believed that such time spent forming one's thought patterns will produce that which is envisioned.

We want to determine when it is according to God's will and when this power is used wrongly. Therefore, we will bring in our understanding of metron and God-given authority. Though we last quoted a Bible passage referring to an evil exercising of power, do not lose sight of our goal of discovering when the Christian *should* use such authority.

This authority should be exercised in line with an individual's metron. For example, think about a Christian named Bill who had a terrible inferiority complex. Because of his past experiences and training, Bill had a difficult time holding down a job or even communicating with other people. Bill went to counseling and over the course of two years, Bill's pastor helped him to develop new thought patterns. Whenever Bill faces a challenging situation today, he meditates on the promises of God and such Bible verses as, "I can do all things through Him who strengthens me" (Phil. 4:13). Bill is now living a productive life, and he no longer struggles with thoughts of inferiority, as he did during his earlier years.

Bill has succeeded at manipulating the visions and thoughts in his mind. Is this right? Of course it is. God gave him authority over his own life, and he should do what is necessary to succeed.

It is important to note that Bill was dealing within his own metron, and he was bringing his thoughts into conformity with God's will. The Apostle Paul exhorted Christians to take "every thought captive to the obedience of Christ" (I Cor. 10:5). Bill was doing what the Bible tells us to do.

If, however, a person—Christian or non-Christian—manipulates the visions in his mind beyond their metron or contrary to the will of God, then evil spiritual exercises may be employed. For example, if a person sees himself dominating other people, greedily accumulating wealth, conquering his opponents, ruling over his employer, etc., the issue of usurping authority is raised. Some of the positive-thinking techniques being taught today cross over into evil exercises of spiritual authority. Even Christians are sometimes guilty of wrongly manipulating their own thoughts while they are "praying." Wherever people actively alter the thought patterns in their own minds, they may release spiritual energies.

Those energies will be evil if and when the person has no God-given authority in the related area. What we are saying is that we need to be careful with some of the aggressive battles which we wage in our minds.

The ministries today which are referred to as "inner healing" or "healing of the memories" should be considered here. The standard procedure in such ministries is first of all to help a person remember bad experiences in the past, and then to help them walk through those times in their thoughtlife, all in an effort to let God heal them. Typically, the individual receiving ministry is asked to envision Jesus walking into their life at the moments of crisis, comforting them, and helping them through whatever the trial was. One of the works accomplished through such inner healing ministries is that the person receiving ministry changes his perception of experiences in the past and, hence, acts differently in the present.

Now, some Christians categorically have condemned all such activities as evil. That is not our intent here. In fact, we clearly acknowledge that thousands of people have been healed emotionally and set free by sincere, valid ministries using these methods. The time they are in violation of God's authority is either when they are applied as mechanistic techniques without the leading of the Holy Spirit, or when the visions formed in the mind of the individual are not in line with God's will. Understanding this caution, we need to bless and encourage ministries which, indeed, are helping others think God's thoughts and clean up the wounds and bad memories of the past.

This subject of controlling thoughts has implications beyond one's own personhood or success. There are thought patterns related to other people that also should be taken captive.

For example, if a mother has thoughts about her child being physically hurt, she should do in the natural what she can to assure her child's safety, but she also should cast those thoughts out of her mind. If she continues to focus on her child being harmed, she actually may start believing in her heart that it will happen, and, to some degree, release spiritual forces to cause it. Remember what Jesus taught us—that which we loose is loosed. There may be times when the mother in our example is unable to rid herself of the negative thoughts. In such cases, she should become more forceful, using the Name of Jesus to bind the work of the enemy. It also may be helpful to enlist the support of another Christian, who by agreeing in prayer more powerfully can diffuse the strategies of Satan. By aggressively rejecting evil thoughts, the mother will bring peace of mind to herself and bind evil from coming upon her child.

Similarly, a person will release blessings upon other people simply by believing the best about them. If negative thoughts about other people are rising constantly, then a person may have to assertively and aggressively reject those impressions. The Apostle Paul explained that he chose to recognize no man according to the flesh but to see them as God sees them (II Cor. 5:16). We are not talking about being naive or blinding ourselves to the evils of other people, but we simply are teaching the biblical principle of controlling our own thoughts toward others.

These truths also have implications for the whole world of the spirit. As we mentioned earlier, people can influence the activities of spirit-beings by manipulating the visions within their mind. Sometimes long seasons of prayer accompanied by fasting can release tremendous forces in the spiritual realm to accomplish that which is fixed in the mind. However, not all such exercises are in line with God's will. This issue is so important, we would like to address it more clearly in Chapter 9, when we talk about out-of-body experiences.

We need to understand that *by manipulating the visions in our mind and authoritatively rejecting certain thoughts, we are exercising spiritual authority.* That is great and should be encouraged when a person is moving within their own metron. However, it is wrong if a person extends his spirit beyond that which God has ordained for his life at present.

There are some non-Christian teachings today which take the principles of thought manipulation so far as to claim that a person can "create his own reality." By this, they mean that a person who carefully controls his every thought and only thinks upon what he desires in life, literally will change the world around him to conform to his images. For example, a woman who is living in a home where her husband physically and emotionally abuses her may be told to create her own reality with her thoughts. She may be taught that if she sees her husband as loving and gentle, he eventually will become what she believes. Another example is of the man who is in serious financial trouble, and he is taught to think of himself as wealthy and having no difficulties.

Again, we emphasize that our thoughts influence the emanation of our spirit, and that our spiritual energy influences this world. However, it is wrong, deceptive, and dangerous to go so far as to say that we can "create our own reality" simply by thinking right.

There are many people in mental institutions today who think they are something which they are not. The insane man who jumps off a roof will crash to the ground, no matter how much he envisions himself flying. Likewise, the woman to whom we referred who is trapped in an abusive home should try to keep a positive attitude, but she also needs to face reality and get practical help. The man in financial trouble must not be allowed to deny his difficulties. That is not faith. That is not Christian. Certainly, he should be encouraged to believe God and even to renew his mind to the fact that he can overcome his troubles through the help and guidance of Jesus

Christ. *But he must not deny reality nor use positive-thinking principles as an excuse not to work hard and pay off those bills.*

Some Christians have misunderstood the principles of faith and gone so far as to live their lives denying reality. The Bible clearly tells us that faith without works is dead (James 2:26). We influence the world around us not merely by *thinking* but by determining God's will and then by acting in faith. Thoughts which hinder us from acting correctly should be cast down (yes, manipulated in our minds). Thoughts contrary to God's thoughts must be overcome. Then we will have the spiritual energy to act and change this natural world.

In all mind-renewing principles, we need to recognize where the power originates. Sometimes people will think of any good results as coming from the mechanism itself. Of course, there is power in the human spirit itself, and controlling thoughts will release that power. However, the Christian should be renewing his mind to the Word of God. It is God's power which abides within His words (Heb. 4:12; II Tim. 3:16-17; Rom. 1:16). When the Christian meditates on God's Word, God's blessings are released (Ps. 1:2-3).

For example, take a Christian named Joe who envisions an imaginary sword sweeping across his mind cutting away from him negative thoughts. He may experience some level of freedom, but, typically, the battle in his mind will be continuous because he is releasing only the power of his own human spirit. If a devil has been involved in tormenting his mind the victory will be even less enduring. Even Jesus Christ used the Word of God to defeat the temptations of Satan (Luke 4:1-12). The Sword which Joe must use, therefore, is the Word of God (Eph. 6:17). If Joe renews his mind to God's Word and spends time meditating on the Bible, he will be releasing God's authority. Devils must bow and the natural world yields to the Kingdom of God.

What we are emphasizing is that there is substance within God's words. That substance contains the power of God. The words themselves are living and active and sharp (Heb. 4:12). The believer is not left with merely the power of the human spirit. He must ingest within his spirit the words of God. Then mind-renewing principles are divinely powerful (II Cor. 10:3-5).

We can summarize this by saying that the Christian should bring his own thoughts in line with God's. Sometimes this even requires an assertive stance in the spirit whereby contrary thoughts are forcefully rejected. This authority should be exercised over everything pertaining to an individual's own metron. He should think positively about his future and his past. He should reject thoughts of condemnation, negativity, and failure. He also should think positively about other people and the world around him. When a Christian asserts authority in this fashion over the thoughts within his own mind, he releases the spiritual energy within him according to the will of God. When meditating upon the words of God, God's power flows out accordingly.

Out-of-body Experiences

As we mentioned earlier, it is from the Bible that we get the terminology, *out-of-body experience.* It was the Apostle Paul who explained that he was taken up into heaven, "whether in the body or out of the body," he was not sure (II Cor. 12:2-3). Of course, there are many such phenomena reported in the non-Christian context today. However, there is much deception involved with these experiences. Let's determine what is true and what is false.

Witches often are pictured as riding on a broom, which is a symbol referring to their practice of sending their spirit to another location. The medicine men of certain primitive peoples and those deep in the use of black magic are said to be able to send their spirit into other places and then "watch" what is going on at those locations.

There has been all kinds of folklore developed around the mystical stories of witches, warlocks, and medicine men. The Christian would be naive to believe most of them. What they actually can do is clouded by the fact that things in the spiritual realm are not perceived as logical, accurate information. As we explained (Volume I, Chapter 2), the spirit perceives things in the forms of impulses, words, visions, impressions, etc. When a witch, therefore, sends her spirit to another place, that which is perceived does not come to her in clear thought patterns as we typically understand. Her mind is only in a semiconscious state. All impressions received must be interpreted, and images are only partial, at best. Stories that have developed from the evil use of this power are exaggerated very easily. In addition, because the witch is exercising authority beyond that which God has given her, demonic activity typically is involved. Satan, who is the father of lies (John 8:44), distorts visions and spiritual reality any way he can for his own purposes. Witches and others who attempt to operate in the spiritual realm typically are very deceived about what they themselves are accomplishing and perceiving.

Another evil form of spirit emanation being used today is called *transcendental meditation*. Some advocates have tried to remove some of the magical, mystical elements associated with witchcraft, but similar techniques are used. Various forms of transcendental meditation are sometimes presented today under the guise of scientific investigations, and they currently are being taught in some universities and high schools as a part of normal classroom activity.

It is helpful to identify what actually is happening in such spiritual exercises. First, we should ask, "What leaves the physical body in these experiences? Is it the spirit or the soul?" When non-Christians try to address this question they offer many confusing answers because they do not even understand the difference between the spirit and the soul (Vol. II, Chapters 1 and 2). They sometimes refer to their practices as *soul travel,* when they really are engaged in spirit emanation. Having no Bible basis to understand man's nature, they rarely know what takes place during such experiences of their own. Let's identify what actually is taking place.

In preceding chapters, we have been discussing various emanations of a person's spirit, that is, the spiritual energy within them reaching out of their soul and body, to touch other people, places, or things. When Paul wrote to the Corinthians and Colossians that he was with them in spirit, he was not referring to his soul being in a different location than his body. No. It was his spiritual influence.

In some situations, it is possible for a person's soul to be in a different location than their body. These are not as common. In fact, we have been explaining the emanation of the human spirit as an everyday experience for every human being. However, the soul reaching out of the human body is much more infrequent, and most people may never experience this during their lifetime.

When Paul was taken up into Paradise, he was not sure whether he was in the body or out of the body. Such terminology implies that he himself, spirit and soul (maybe even bodily), was lifted into the throne room of God. When a person's soul is taken to another location, he will experience that new location to some degree as if he were present physically in that place. He will see it or touch it or experience it in some tangible way. On the other hand, if only his spirit is reaching out, he will be completely unaware of it, or at best, have a mere intuitive feeling concerning what is happening in that other location or with the people there.

Another point for our understanding concerns the dimension in which a person's spirit or soul travels. Non-Christians involved in projecting their spirit and/or soul often describe their activities as *astral projection*. By this terminology, they are referring to a person sending their spirit or soul out of their body through a spiritual dimension, which they refer to as an *astral plane*.

This terminology is deceiving. When they use the phrase *astral plane*, they are implying that there is a spiritual dimension out there which is much like a road on which we could drive our cars. It is true that the spiritual dimension is real, but we must not see it as neutral grounds on which people can travel safely.

As a Bible-believing Christian, I would rather refer to that spiritual dimension as the "second heaven" (or "the heavenlies"). We understand that the third heaven is Paradise, where

God Himself dwells (II Cor. 12:2-4). In contrast, the first heaven is the natural realm above us, including the sky, the clouds, the stars, and everything you can see as you look up at night or during the day. If you stepped outside and looked up, we would say you are looking at the first heaven. It is the "second heaven" which we understand as *the spiritual dimension encompassing and superimposed upon this natural world.* It is in the second heaven that angels and devils interact. It is not up in the highest realm where God dwells in unapproachable light. Nor is it the natural sky or stars. But it is the spiritual world corresponding to the natural world in which we live.

Most of the spiritual activity about which we have been talking occurs neither in the third heaven (where God's throne room is), nor in the natural heavens. The spirits of men primarily exist in the second heaven. When a person projects their spirit and/or soul, they are projecting it through the second heaven.

When people project their spirits and/or soul, they are not traveling a neutral, abandoned "astral plane." No. They are sending a part of themselves into a world in which spirit-beings act, a world where definite territories and authority structures exist. Satan has established his kingdom there, and God's angels are also at work in that realm.

When a person lets his spirit flow out over his own God-given metron, he is not violating authority. However, when a person projects his spirit through the second heaven beyond his metron, he is crossing authority lines. It is dangerous. Demonic powers have the authority to hurt people there. And they do.

It is not only demons which may be encountered. God has spirit-beings which also deserve respect. When Elisha's servant had his eyes opened, he saw into the spiritual realm and beheld the mountain around filled with horses and chariots of fire (II Kings 6:17). For another example, look at what Ezekiel saw: four living beings in the middle of spinning wheels with fire and lightning flashing forth (Ezek. 1:1-14). The wheels, we are told, extend all the way from the surface of the earth to the throne room of God above. A terrifying sight it was to Ezekiel. However, it was just as terrifying for the Apostle John to see in the spiritual realm some of the beings which serve God, as he recorded in the book of Revelation.

What we need to realize is that *when a person extends his spirit and/or soul into the second heaven, he is crossing established authority structures and may be violating those authority lines.*

An example of such violations can be seen in the passage we read earlier from the book of Jude:

> And angels who did not keep
> their own domain...as
> Sodom and Gomorrah and
> the cities around them...in
> the same manner these
> men, also by dreaming, de-
> file the flesh, and reject au-
> thority, and revile angelic
> majesties (Jude, vs. 6-8).

These evil men were going beyond their authority, like angels who do not "keep their own domain." By dreaming, in the sense of manipulating the visions within their own minds, they were challenging spirit entities.

This passage is referring primarily to evil men who envision themselves as conquering kingdoms, oppressing other peoples, or dominating areas which God has not given to them. As people manipulate the visions in their minds in such fashion, they actually may exert forces upon established authorities, angels or devils.

Similar violations can happen by well-meaning Christians. For example, if an intercessory team begins praying against some spiritual force, and as they do so they begin to see certain evil spirit-beings bow to them, they actually may be exerting forces upon devils which exist in the second heaven. Those devils may indeed bow, especially if there is unity among the intercessors and/or they have united their hearts through intense fasting and extended periods of prayer.

We are not condemning all such intercessory prayer. What we are doing is teaching how to stay within the limits of God-given authority. Prayer warriors should boldly take and hold the spiritual territory which God already has given to them. They should also move into new areas as they sense the Holy Spirit leading them.

However, it is the overzealous, even arrogant challenges against the devil which we must warn Christians to avoid. It is wrong and dangerous.

Jude went on to explain:

> But Michael the archangel, when he disputed with the devil and argued about the body of Moses, did not dare pronounce against him a railing judgment, but said, "The Lord rebuke you." But these men revile the things which they do not understand; and the things which they know by instinct, like unreasoning animals, by these things they are destroyed. Woe to them! (Jude, vs. 6-11a).

Notice that the people who engage in such spiritual violations of authority even may be "destroyed" by those spirit-beings whom they revile.

We can see this truth in operation in the world today. When a person projects his spirit into the second heaven, where he has no authority, incredibly wicked demonic encounters can occur. Devils may come to use the person for their own benefit, or they simply may come to steal, kill, and destroy. Deception often creeps in. Thought patterns frequently become twisted. The spirit of the man may be projected to such a great extent that the spiritual energy left in his mind is diminished, and rational thought no longer is possible. Bizarre behavior patterns sometimes become established in those involved in such activities. There are many people in mental institutions today as a result of such encounters. Sometimes a person's spirit will leave his body to such a degree that there is no longer enough spiritual energy resident within his body to maintain physical and/or mental health. Those stepping into Satan's territory are open targets for his wicked schemes.

Even evil people who teach others how to project their spirit and/or soul are aware of some of the related dangers. Witches are known to experience sudden attacks of illness and emotional torment. People involved in transcendental meditation commonly go through periods of depression, collapse of relationships, and financial disaster. There are several books written by New Age advocates giving testimonies of people who have suffered tremendously after going too far in such spiritual exercises. Although these groups do not stop their evil activities, they are somewhat aware of the dangers and sometimes even warn their own trainees to beware.

If the heathens who do not know God are cautious, how much more should the Christian who believes the Bible be wise to these truths? As a person exalts himself beyond his metron, he extends himself beyond God's protection and, therefore, opens himself to demonic activity. This warning is for the Christian and the non-Christian.

It is true that God sometimes will carry a person through the second heaven. He has authority to do so. When the Holy Spirit initiates it, the person is safe. To be in God's will is to be within His protection.

There are many examples in the Bible of second-heaven experiences. Most of the supernatural experiences which we already have given occurred within the second heaven. To read more examples, all one has to do is thumb through the pages of the Old Testament prophets and pick out phrases that talk about visions, or of being taken to another place. For example Ezekiel wrote:

> In the visions of God He
> brought me into the land of

> Israel, and set me on a very high mountain... (Ezek. 40:2);
>
> Then he brought me to the porch of the temple... (Ezek. 40:48);
>
> The hand of the Lord was upon me, and He brought me out by the Spirit of the LORD and set me down in the middle of the valley... (Ezek. 37:1).

There are several similar accounts in the New Testament of second-heaven experiences (e.g., Acts 10:3-7; 10:9-20; 16:9; the Book of Rev.).

Understanding that it is only within God's authority that we act, as Christians we do want to be open to second-heaven experiences. When a Christian today yields to the Holy Spirit, he, too, may find himself being taken to another place spiritually. As we mentioned earlier, intercessors extend their spiritual influence to those for whom they pray, but they also may go a step further and actually be taken to another location in spirit and/or soul. Many believers also have been carried to other locations while worshipping God.

Such experiences are true and should not be rejected. They should be judged even as all revelations and spiritual phenomenon should be (I

Cor. 14:29-32). But we, as Bible-believing people, must be open to all the works of God. Our point is that God is the God of the second heaven, and any man who takes it upon himself to travel there is stepping beyond personal authority. However, if God, by the Holy Spirit, takes a Christian through such an experience, let God be God.

A final point worth mentioning is that people often project their spirits into forbidden areas of the spirit-world unconsciously. Many have pierced the heavens through intense meditation. Others have lost touch with this world by slipping into their own imaginations. Still others end up drifting into the spirit as a result of sudden breaks in relationships with other people. For example, a person who is bonded closely in marriage or to a certain group of individuals at some time may experience complete rejection. As a consequence, his own spirit may lose contact with those people. Then if bitterness or anger sets in, that person may turn his heart with such force that his spirit is carried away like a kite on the wind. Of course, we are speaking only in terms of comparisons here, but we need to understand that many people, perhaps most, who experience destructive second-heaven encounters, enter in without realizing what they are doing.

Proverbs 25:28 tells us:

> Like a city that is broken
> into and without walls

Is a man who has no control
over his own spirit.

The person who projects his spirit out into the spiritual world, and lets his spirit wander out there, is like an unprotected city. He is unclothed. He is naked and open for attack. Don't allow that to happen in your life.

10
Through Space and Time

What we want to investigate now is how things may be experienced at a distance as one's spirit and/or soul touches the related locations. First, we will consider the experiences through space and then through time.

We have made a distinction between spirit emanation and soul travel. Both entail a portion of a person's being leaving his physical body and reaching to another location. We will not make that distinction in the following discussion; however, keep in mind that if one's soul touches another location, it will be a much "fuller" experience. When one's spirit reaches out, the individual usually is not even aware of what is occurring but on occasion may have an intuitive impression concerning that other place. We can compare the spirit of a man with a film projector which projects images and spiritual impressions upon the screen of a man's soul. The soul is conscious of that with which the spirit has contact, if it is focused and receptive to the spirit (Vol. 1, Chapter 2-4). Those impressions are vague and may never be noticed. However, if the entire soul of an individual leaves his body, it will be a much more impacting and memorable experience.

In the Bible, we can read of several rather amazing incidents of people perceiving things at a location removed from their physical body. We already looked at Second Kings 5, where the prophet Elisha confronted his servant Gehazi after Gehazi left the prophet and committed an evil deed. The prophet said to Gehazi upon his return:

> "Did not my heart go with you, when the man turned from his chariot to meet you?" (II Kings 5:26).

The eyes of the prophet's heart "watched" what happened. His spirit literally went out with the servant, and Elisha, who was located physically in another place, became conscious of his servant's act.

The prophet Daniel had many such experiences. One of several recorded in the Book of Daniel reads like this:

> And I looked in the vision, and it came about while I was looking, that I was in the citadel of Susa, which is in the province of Elam; and I looked in the vision, and I

myself was beside the Ulai
Canal (Dan. 8:2).

Daniel had been taken by the Spirit of God to a
distant location, and he saw as if he actually
were present there.

Ezekiel, similarly, tells of such experiences:

And the Spirit lifted me up
and brought me in a vision
by the Spirit of God to the
exiles in Chaldea (Ezek.
11:24a).

In the New Testament, we can read about the
Apostle Paul being opened to see a vision of a
Macedonian man appealing to him to come and
preach there (Acts 9-10). Similarly, Peter was
told by the Holy Spirit that there were three men
looking for him, and he was supposed to go to
them (Acts 10:19-20).

Jesus demonstrated this "perception at a distance" in several instances. One example is given
in John 1:46-50, where we read about our Lord
meeting Nathanael for the first time. As
Nathanael came to greet Jesus, our Lord declared what Nathanael was like in character.
When Nathanael inquired of Jesus how He knew
these things, Jesus said:

"Before Philip called you,
when you were under the fig

tree, I saw you" (John 1:48b).

Jesus said that He "saw" Nathanael, even though he was at a distant location.

Each of these examples from the Bible, as well as any such present-day experiences, could be explained as a sovereign work of the Holy Spirit, and we, as Christians, could understand that in each incident the Holy Spirit simply is coming upon a person and revealing that which He wants them to know. It is good to give credit to the Spirit of God in such cases, and He often does intervene sovereignly in the affairs of men to reveal that which cannot be known through natural means (I Cor. 2:12-13).

However, the biblical understanding we have been developing throughout these volumes points to the fact that the spirit itself which is in man has the ability to perceive things. We discover these abilities at work in both the Christian's and non-Christian's lives. These senses do not open only by the sovereign work of the Holy Spirit. We have been trying to emphasize the reality of how the individual's spirit can reveal things to him. Of course, we recognize a sovereign God who is at work within us and outside of us. But we hope believers understand that God has given them a spirit, just as He has given them a physical body. The spirit has senses just as does the body. The spirit itself can hear, see, and perceive things (Vol. I, Chapter 2). That is how God created us.

Remember that every human being has a spirit which is not limited to the confines of his body. Every human being has a spirit which emanates from him. A businessman who accepts responsibility for his business is sending out his spirit all the time. The pastor who cares for his sheep is bathing those people in the realm of the spirit. Every time a person talks with authority, he is emitting spiritual energy.

Every human being also senses things with which his spirit has contact. For example, consider the mother who is asleep at home when her daughter gets in an automobile accident across town. Even though that daughter is miles away, the mother may be awakened suddenly, knowing something tragic has happened.

People often feel the pains and troubles of those to whom they are bonded spiritually, even when they are distant. The Bible tells us that when one part of the Body of Christ hurts, we all hurt (I Cor. 12:26). Married couples often sense what their mate is experiencing before anything has been communicated in the natural. People sense things about their children, even if those loved ones are miles away. It is very common for people to react and respond to others spiritually before they do naturally.

Many individuals have experienced a "knowing" concerning others, especially if those other people have their heart turned toward them. For example, when the telephone rings, some individuals have an amazing ability to know who it is that is calling them. If someone is about to meet them unannounced, they will be thinking about that person immediately preceding the encounter. These types of spirit contacts are common, and all of us experience them to some degree.

Not only does the spirit sense at a distance *things* related to other people, but also to *events, circumstances, opportunities,* and *objects.* For example, a businessman who accepts responsibility for his business at times may have things about his business being revealed to him by no naturally understood means. A real estate investor often will have a "gut feeling" about some possible investment ahead of him. An administrator who is organizing a huge upcoming event may experience an uneasiness concerning that which needs more attention and work. A mother may feel her children, left in another room of the house, making a complete mess of things. People regularly base decisions on what often is called instinct or intuition. Many such sensings are real impressions which a person's spirit is perceiving at a distance.

A very common experience shared by many people today is how they perceive things with their spirit as they drive their automobile. People who do much long-distance driving tend to relax and confidently sit back while they are traveling down the road. In such a posture of soul, we understand that their spirit may reach out ahead of them. The spirit then becomes involved in the driving process in such a way that if a car suddenly stops ahead of them, or danger appears on the road, their spirit senses it before their eyes do and they first are alerted spiritually. In many such incidents, people are brought to attention just before it is too late. The danger initially was perceived by the spirit.

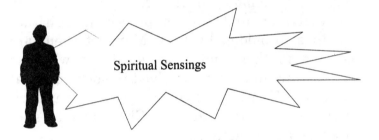

Spiritual Sensings

We already have discussed how the spirit reveals the thoughts of a man. In relationship to the emanating spirit, we can understand that the spirit of a man will reach out and fill his metron, if he accepts responsibility for it. His spirit then is going to have contact with his area of God-given authority. Of course, God is the only One who can delegate true authority, but when God delegates to a man a certain metron, that person will have the spiritual ability to manage it. His spirit will emanate outward and project back to the conscious mind that which it perceives. Every individual will know things about his own metron through his spirit.

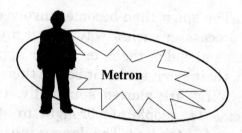

I am trying to enlighten you that such experiences of sensing things at a distance are not necessarily demonic in nature. Of course, there are evil men and women practicing spiritual sensings forbidden by God. Many of them are assisted in their endeavors by devils who are very willing to become involved in such spiritual exercises. We are not giving approval to any such practices, and we warn all Christians to stay away from such activities.

However, we also recognize that the spirit which God put within man is capable of sensing things pertaining to distant locations. That is how God made us. *Every human being is influenced and directed, to some extent, by that which his spirit is receiving.* It is foolish and contrary to biblical truth to categorize all spiritual sensings as evil.

I have heard stories of Christians who have experienced some supernatural phenomenon, and when they tried to share the experience with some person in their church whom they respect, they were told never to talk about it and to deny it, so that it never would happen again. For example, Tom, a Christian man, told me that years earlier he saw a vision of a person stranded on a snowmobile near his snow-laden home. He went to investigate as the vision had been shown to him. Sure enough, he found an individual in need and he was able to help. When Tom went to tell the leaders of his church what had happened, they told him that it was a devil communicating to him. He spent the next several years feeling guilty and trying to deny his experience. That was, of course, until he met me.

Obviously, you have figured out by now that I am presenting a new look at the spiritual realm. At this point you either must be upset with me or you are rejoicing to hear these truths. I trust the second is your response.

We can take one step further into these truths by saying that a person's spirit also may touch things belonging to another time period. Not only does our spirit have the ability to reach to another physical location, but also to another location in time.

The most obvious examples are of how the prophets in the Bible saw the future. When prophets such as Jeremiah, Ezekiel, Daniel, and Isaiah prophesied, they often would describe visions that they were seeing, and their words were stated as if they were watching the future as it happened. For example, they might describe the birth of Jesus hundreds of years before it actually occurred.

It is unclear whether such prophetic experiences were the result of the *prophet's* spirit reaching into the future, or of *God's* Spirit bringing a vision of the future into their spirit which is located in the present. Either way, the results are identical: the spirit of the prophet is receiving information belonging to a time not yet arrived.

In the Book of Acts, we read about the prophet Agabus perceiving the future on two different occasions. In Acts 11:27-28, we are told about his foretelling a coming famine. In Acts 21:10-14, Agabus tells Paul about the imprisonment awaiting him in Jerusalem. Paul said:

> "And now, behold, bound in spirit, I am on my way to Jerusalem, not knowing what will happen to me there, except that the Holy Spirit solemnly testifies to me in every city, saying that bonds and afflictions await me" (Acts 20:22-23).

Notice that the Apostle mentioned how "in every city" the Holy Spirit would warn him about the future. It was, therefore, a fairly common experience for Paul to have some inclination about what was ahead of him. In Paul's experiences, and the two recorded of Agabus, the Holy Spirit is given credit for revealing the future events.

We believe that such sensings of the future are more common than most Christians have allowed themselves to believe. The whole topic of transcending time is taboo in many Christian circles today. This is due partly to the evil, occultic exercises in this area, and partly because of a fear which keeps Christians from actually looking in the Bible to see if these things are true. Now, we are declaring that such experiences are true and valid, and not automatically evil.

Our concern is whether it is God or Satan who is behind such activities. It is our understanding that God is the only One with authority over time. God's fundamental declaration of Himself, "I AM", is, among other things, a statement of His existence throughout eternity, past and future. Jesus Himself declared, "...before Abraham was born, I am" (John 8:58). God has authority over all. Time is within His metron. As we stated earlier, created beings were created within the context of time. They have been assigned to the present. Man's metron is now.

However, there may be occasions when men, on God's initiation, do sense things in the future (and in the past, as we will mention shortly). We already have referred to the prophet's experience of this, but let's mention a few others.

Some Christians, for example, who are deeply involved in a church, frequently know in advance what that group of Christians will be doing next. Often before a church service, a certain Christian may be reading his Bible, and then when he arrives at church, he discovers that the pastor is going to preach on the very Bible passages he was led to read earlier. We explain this phenomenon as the Christian becoming one with the Holy Spirit who is guiding that group of Christians.

In some inner healing ministries, the minister will be praying for the counselee, and he will begin to see visions of what happened in the past. The Holy Spirit may reveal how the person was hurt emotionally or perhaps rejected years earlier. These are true words of knowledge given by the Holy Spirit.

Another example of transcending time is when God reveals to a person something about to happen, as He did with the prophets. John Alexander Dowie was a famous minister in America around the turn of the Nineteenth Century. He had several thousand people looking to him for leadership; he also had some enemies. On one occasion, while he was sleeping he had a vision of a bomb going off in his office. Later he went to his office, but left early believing that God had warned him. Sure enough, the explosion would have killed him had he not heeded the vision given to him earlier.

There are many, many accounts of missionaries who have been warned of some impending danger through visions. If we were to compile some of the stories, we could fill several books.

There are also experiences of the future outside the Christian context, which we would not consider evil. Here we are *not* talking about a palmreader's attempt at reading someone's future, *nor* the astrologer's endeavor to perceive the future by gazing into the stars. Those activities are undoubtedly evil and condemned in the Bible (Deut. 18:10-12). Please do not think we are giving credence to any such practices.

Consider the engineer who designs and oversees the construction of a huge bridge. If he has a premonition of that bridge collapsing, we need not jump to the conclusion that he is having problems with devils. Perhaps a devil is involved and is just trying to discourage him. In such cases, those thoughts should be rejected aggressively. But it also may be true that his human spirit simply is sensing a danger. He would be wise in that case to investigate and see if, indeed, a genuine problem has been perceived spiritually.

Many people also have had experiences of knowing the future in very small practical ways. An example is when a person sets the alarm clock to waken at a time different than his regularly scheduled time. In the morning, one instant before the alarm sounds, he wakes up to turn it off. His spirit sensed what was about to happen.

Many people have had the experience which we call "*deja vu.*" A person will be performing their normal activities and suddenly feel as if they already have experienced everything around them. It is as if they are re-living that exact time period. Our understanding of this is that the person's spirit at an earlier time reached into the future and "tasted of the things to come." This is not a conscious endeavor, but it simply happens because our spirit has this ability.

We want to emphasize that such spiritual sensing of the future or past are not always evil. They can be. Of course, the devil at times may be involved. I am suspicious of any such exercises done by a person with known occultic involvement. A person with past experiences in evil spiritual exercises or drugs can have demonically inspired visions for years afterward. We must discern and judge all things (I Thess. 5:21).

However, we must not reject them all categorically. It is by God's design that man was created with a spirit. That spirit is assigned to a time, but on occasion it may sense something ahead. *No man has the authority to try to transcend time by an act of his own will. Such activity is a violation of God's authority.* However, we also understand that God made us with a spirit, and sometime it senses things ahead within our own metron. Also, the God of all time can and does allow people to see things belonging to another time, as He so chooses.

Finally, let's add a warning concerning what some have experienced related to a *confusion of time.* For example, there was a famous Christian leader by the name of William Branham who ministered mostly in the 1950's and early 60's. He was known for his ability to perceive things in the spirit world and was especially gifted in revealing the name of people unknown to him. This man, who was incredibly gifted by God, also had some serious misunderstandings.

For example, he began to believe and teach that man pre-existed the creation of this earth. William Branham began teaching that all people lived eternally, and that when it is our time to be born, we simply descend out of heaven into our mother's womb to be born in a physical body. This doctrine, called the pre-existence of man, has some serious implications which contradict basic Christian beliefs. The main contradiction comes from Branham's thinking that if man always existed, then he always had a will, and, therefore, he was either good or bad before this world was created. Believing this, William Branham had to conclude that every human being comes into this world with a pre-determined bent toward good or evil. The problem with this thinking is that it changes the fundamental purpose of Jesus' death and resurrection. William Branham had to conclude that "good people" merely *discover* Jesus while they are alive on this earth, then go back to be with Him. On the other hand, "bad people" reject Jesus. This way of thinking leaves no place for the foundational Christian belief that sinful man finds forgiveness in Jesus and then enters a process of becoming transformed into His image.

Although such doctrinal errors may be subtle at first, they have profound, far-reaching implications. For this reason, we must judge all spiritual experiences on the basis of the written Word of God, the exaltation of Jesus as Lord, and the fruit borne over the long range.

This is especially important when talking about spiritual experiences related to time and space. When the prophets in the Old Testament perceived facts about the coming birth of Jesus, they usually did not know what time period they were perceiving. It is also true that people today may go into the realm of the spirit and become confused concerning what time period they are sensing. It is helpful to compare such experiences with an individual coming out of a deep sleep— for a moment or two, they may be confused as to where they are or what the date is. In similar fashion, people who tap into the spirit world often experience a confusion concerning when they exist (and who they are, which will be discussed in Volume 7).

In William Branham's case, he started to believe that he existed before this world was created. It is true that he may have gone into the spiritual world and experienced to some degree the foundations of this world. Perhaps he even tasted of God's thoughts about mankind when we were conceived only in God's Spirit. However, we must reject the idea that mankind existed then.

11

Understanding Dreams

With the understanding that we have developed concerning the human spirit, we now can explain the function and role that dreams can play. We do not intend to discuss everything involved in dreams in this chapter. That would be as foolish as trying to explain in just a few pages everything which the human body does. At this point, simply a basic understanding will help us.

The spirit of a man does not sleep. It is *always willing,* even though the flesh is weak (Matt. 26:41). While the body rests, the spirit remains active. In fact, it is even more free in its activities because conscious thoughts are detached from it. The individual is exerting less strict authority over his spirit while asleep.

During sleep, people receive information from all with which their spirit is having contact. Even though their minds are detached from the natural world, their spirit continues to flow outward. That which the spirit contacts is projected back to the soul and often appears as images upon the mind. This causes many different visual experiences.

At times, the images seem entirely disjointed and meaningless, but they are not. While we dream, our spirit draws in all sorts of information. We could compare it with how our natural senses would perceive many things if we were standing high on top of a mountain surveying the countryside. A difference, though, is that *our spirit draws in information from both the natural and spiritual worlds.*

From the spiritual realm, sleeping people often perceive things related to angelic or demonic activity. If an evil presence passes through a home, a sleeping person may sense it. More than once I have been asked to pray over a person's home because they were having bad dreams. In one of the worst cases, the woman of the house was waking up night after night screaming. It was no surprise when we learned that the person who had lived in the house prior to them had committed suicide. After praying and taking authority over the situation, the home was cleaned out and dreams became peaceful. Pure and holy dreams typically are prevalent in a godly atmosphere.

It is also common for people to know some of the activities going on around them in the natural world, even if they are asleep. For example, sleeping people may incorporate into their dreams activities going on around them, such as a dog walking through the house, or a burglar breaking in, or a television show that is playing beyond hearing distance at the other end of the house. Such experiences reveal to us how the spirit is in touch with the natural world in ways that even our natural senses never are.

Dreams are also very much influenced by the people with whom our spirit has contact. For example, family members, friends, co-workers and the people to whom we are bonded spiritually are likely to appear in our dreams regularly. It is common for a child's dreams to correspond to their parents' spiritual condition. It is also true that if a person with great authority is sleeping nearby, say in the motel room next to yours, you may find yourself receiving images which his spirit is giving off. Whether people are tied together spiritually or by proximity, their spirits influence each other during the night.

Often visions of the night reflect events that happened throughout the person's daily activities. One's spirit is still in touch with those things. Especially stressful events will hold the person's spiritual attention longer. Images of the people involved in those various events may appear throughout the night.

One of the processes happening while a person is receiving images during their sleep is that his spirit is resolving problems related to those images.

We can see this if we add to our understanding how the authority of man emanates from his spirit. When God spoke over mankind, "Fill the earth and subdue it," He imparted into the spirit of man the authority to manage his own life and metron. Because of this abiding authority, the spirit of a person constantly is arising from within him, helping him to have dominion in all the areas concerning his life.

When a problem during the day has not been resolved, the spirit within a person will continue to flow through their mind in an attempt to develop the needed answers. A person may dream a certain dream for several nights, or even weeks in a row, until the spirit within has enough strength to give the person the related authority.

For example, a person who is starting a new job on a factory assembly line may have dreams about his work for several nights in a row. Not understanding what is happening, he may become frustrated and try harder to sleep without being bothered by those dreams. In reality, those night visions are for his benefit. The spirit within him is rising, and it is trying to "take dominion" of the new tasks he is facing. The person may have several nights during which he seems to fail miserably in his dreams. Then, after a season of those dreams, he will find himself more efficient and successful on the job. Because the spirit within him has had enough time to rise up, he then can function better. His body works better. He thinks more clearly. He has strength to last through the day.

People often find themselves able to handle new responsibilities only after they have finished dreaming about them. Once they have succeeded in their dreams, those dreams no longer occur. The spirit within them has then finished doing the necessary work. New avenues of spiritual energy are flowing through the person, making him able to handle the tasks ahead. And the person's spirit is then flowing out to influence the circumstances, events, and people involved.

For similar reasons, a person who is trying to learn a foreign language may dream in that language, but only after he has mastered the language to some degree. When a person begins to dream in another language, that is evidence that the language is now his.

The spirit of a man constantly is rising within him, releasing life energies to keep him healthy, strong, thinking right, and effective in this world. Often the problems being resolved through dreams may deal with difficulties which arose years earlier. For example, a certain woman may have undergone a terrible relationship problem when she was a young girl. Such events can be so devastating that she is unable to deal with the hurt, rejection, and misunderstandings. Her spirit, therefore, may bury the related thoughts until a later time when she is mature and strong enough to handle them. Then when this particular woman is old enough to deal with the past, her spirit may bring it back to her in dreams. Her spirit then will be able to begin resolving the related issues, re-evaluate what actually happened, and align thoughts and feelings in ways that can be incorporated into her whole system of thought.

As the spirit within a person flows freely during sleep, it searches through the mind and bathes the memories and thought patterns. This performs an important function. Since the spirit provides the energy which allows people to think, it is essential that new energy be supplied to the mind on an ongoing basis. The spirit "searches" the mind: "For who among men knows the thoughts of a man except the spirit of the man, which is within him" (I Cor. 2:11a). As it searches and scans through the mind, the spirit re-energizes thoughts and memories which are still important and believed by that individual. However, if information is no longer needed or certain ways of thinking have changed, the related thoughts are released, that is, allowed to diminish in strength. Thoughts that are not touched by the spirit of man from time to time will disappear completely. So we learn that one of the functions of dreaming is to bathe the mind and reorient its patterns of thought according to present beliefs.

For this reason, a person who is undergoing major changes in life will experience an acceleration in dream activities. Thoughts will seem to flood through his mind at an amazing rate when he is in transition or is being exposed to new ways of thinking. Often thoughts will be linked one to another for future reference, or various forms of "revelation" will come alive. It is the function of the spirit to help us cope and adapt with such changes we all experience.

Another major role played by dreams is related to the function of the human spirit in healing a person within. The spirit and soul may need to be healed of wounds resulting from rejection, abuse, errors made in the past, etc. People also can be wounded within as they watch violent or scary movies. Any stressful experiences can hurt a person within, leaving him in need of healing. That healing may come immediately, or it may take years until the spirit within him is able to rise up with enough force to expel the negative effects.

In this sense, dreams can fulfill the same role for the soul/mind as the human kidney does for the physical body, expelling impurities and cleansing the system. In this process, wounds and difficult memories may surface years after they were inflicted. As these things arise, they can appear upon the screen of the mind in the night. Some people not understanding how this operates become very concerned and even plagued with guilt when they themselves are going through such "a cleansing season" in their lives. They wrongly consider such dreams as signs of present evil, rather than past wounds being healed.

It is important to note here that all these activities of the spirit in the night deal with *spiritual impressions,* not natural ones. This means they cannot be taken literally according to logical thought patterns. For example, an adult who starts dreaming that he was abused by his father years ago should not conclude automatically that he, indeed, was beaten or in any other way physically abused. The spirit projects out *the intensity of the wound*, not the literal accuracy. As a child, a person may have been verbally abused by his father, and to the child the seriousness may be equivalent to being stabbed with a knife. If, however, this child grows up and later dreams that his father stabbed him, we should not conclude that the event actually occurred physically. What is important is that with dreams we are dealing with *impressions of equivalent intensity* left upon the spirit and soul of the individual.

It is normal and healthy for the rivers of life to be flowing constantly out of a person's innermost being. When a person is under spiritual attack, or he simply is depleted of his spiritual strength, he may find his dreamlife influenced accordingly. When a person does not have enough spiritual energy within him to maintain healthy thought patterns, errors of the past can flood his mind. Without spiritual energy he is defenseless. Problems and the intensity of the battle are compounded by demonic activity which often come to condemn a person and accuse him. A healthy person is able to admit to his mistakes and then move on in life. A person depleted of spiritual strength is not. Therefore, if an individual is drained of his own spiritual energy, he may find in the night terrible thoughts flowing through his mind related to his own unworthiness and shortcomings. The wise person learns to identify such negative thought patterns as indicators pointing to the need for rest and rejuvenation.

We should add to our understanding of dreamlife by pointing out that the spirit is still in touch with the physical body of the person, healing, helping, and bathing it. Therefore, a sick person may dream about his illness. When health is seen in dreams, it is a good sign that the body is on the way to recovery.

So, also, the spirit may accommodate certain needs of the physical body. For example, a young man may have sexually stimulating thoughts while asleep (as also a woman may). Those thoughts may be the result of bad images he has put within his mind during the day, but they also may be formed by his spirit in order to cause his physical body to release sexual passions. Most young men experience what sometimes is called a "wet dream," where they become so sexually aroused that their body emits seminal fluid. A man should not feel guilty for such experiences. Of course, we are not making excuses for constant or prolonged sexual dreaming, but some such images are normal and even necessary for the development and maintenance of one's body.

What people eat before going to bed also influences their thoughts at night. Fatty substances seem to cause people to release more authority while they sleep. Certain foods seem to keep people from going into as deep a sleep as they normally should. Spicy foods often activate the mind so that more is experienced and remembered. Cheese is high in the amino acid which intensifies color and imagery. Because of such influences of food, some people have used the terminology "pizza dream" to refer to the thoughts which race rapidly in the night after a meal of pizza.

This phenomenon is another example of how our spirit, soul, and body influence each other. Throughout these writings we have been trying to picture the spirit, soul and body of man as completely *engaged*. Like three gears engaged one to another so that the teeth perfectly intermesh, so also the spirit, soul, and body are engaged so that whatever happens to one part influences the others.

This intermeshing of spirit, soul, and body has some profound implications when talking about dreams. We can consider how the physical body may be changed in subtle or even dramatic ways by the ongoing influence of dreams. One's faith orients one's heart. From the heart flows the spiritual energy within. Therefore, as a person dreams, he may be altering the actual structure and makeup of his physical body.

Concerning this, we gave the example of how a sexual dream may activate sexual organs. We also could consider how a dream inducing fear could accelerate one's heart and stimulate the secretion of certain hormones. Similarly, the spirit of a person may form countless variations of images, each of which triggers different physical responses. The spirit, therefore, plays a significant part in adjusting chemical balances in the body, immune system responses, metabolism, and numerous other physical processes—many of which we know little about today.

It is with this perspective that we view dreams. We must realize the incredible intricacy and far-reaching effects which they may have. *They are spiritual functions which adjust the soul and body of a person and also cause the spiritual energy to flow out of each individual in ways that allow him to be more successful in life.*

There is yet another key role which dreams play. Since the spirit is the "lamp of the Lord" (Prov. 20:27), God may intervene in the flow of spiritual impressions to communicate with people. There are many examples in the Bible, but one of the clearest explanations concerning dreams was given to Job by Elihu. Job had three counselors who gave him questionable advice, but the fourth, Elihu, was inspired by God when he said:

"Indeed God speaks once,
Or twice, yet no one notices it.
In a dream, a vision of the night,
When sound sleep falls on men,
While they slumber in their beds,

Then He opens the ears of men,
And seals their instruction"
(Job 33:14-16).

When God speaks, our spirit responds. Sometimes being foolish men we do not even notice that it is Him talking. Other times, our spirit will be troubled within because of a dream (Dan. 2:1). Or a certain dream will return to us because God speaks "once, or twice."

Since God "gives instructions" to men while they sleep, we need to heed what He is saying. It is not the pizza dream to which we should listen. It is not the mass of spiritual information flowing in every night that needs our attention. Nor is it the ongoing bathing of our thought processes. It is when God has intervened in those flowing spiritual impressions that we should listen.

The meaning to some dreams is very obvious. A person may go to bed wondering how he is supposed to act in a certain situation, and then that night have a dream giving him the answer. Of course, we never should receive a dream that tells us to act contrary to God's nature or His Word. Remember, the devil also can influence our dreams. Visions of the night need to be discerned just like prophecies or any other spiritual messages.

Dreams whose meanings are not obvious need to be interpreted with spiritual understanding. We read in the Bible about Daniel interpreting the dreams of King Nebuchadnezzar and

Joseph interpreting the dreams of Pharaoh and others. Because we are dealing with spiritual impressions, logic or mechanical formulas of interpretation cannot be trusted. Sometimes people who do not understand the spiritual dimension try to develop "rules of interpretation," implying that a certain picture always means some specific thing. It doesn't. There may be some patterns that can be applied, but for the most part *all* "formulas" are faulty. Things which are spiritual can only be discerned spiritually (I Cor. 2:12-14).

What is required for true discernment is spiritual understanding. We are told that Daniel could interpret dreams because:

> "...an extraordinary spirit, knowledge and insight, interpretation of dreams, explanation of enigmas, and solving of difficult problems were found in this Daniel..." (Dan. 5:12; see also Dan. 1:17).

Similarly, Joseph had a gift from God enabling him to interpret dreams.

Now, we do not point out these truths to discourage the average Christian from trying to understand his own dreams. After all, God is communicating with people through dreams. He is not purposely making it impossible for people to understand Him. No. We simply are emphasizing the need for spiritual rather than natural understanding.

In order to interpret a dream, the individual must pay attention to the "impression" upon his spirit. For example, if in the night he receives a picture of himself flying in an airplane, he should interpret that vision in view of how it impacts him personally. An airplane ride to one person can mean an exciting trip, while it means to another person business travel. A different individual may have a terrible fear of airplanes, and therefore, the image of an airplane is a forewarning of upcoming danger which literally has nothing to do with an airplane ride. The person who does not understand spiritual impressions may conclude wrongly that the person who received such a dream soon will go on a trip. The individual sensitive to the spirit will be more in tune with the unique situation of the individual who had the dream.

God communicates in dreams with spiritual impressions. When those spiritual impressions are aligned, then understanding is obtained.

Again, we need to say that we are in no way trying to give an in-depth teaching on dreams or their interpretation. There are other books written on this subject. Although we do not recommend any of the non-Christian writings on such topics, the Church is more and more opening to the reality and significance of spiritual truths like these. The Body of Christ, rather than the heathen, should be at the forefront of understanding such spiritual realities. In the Bible, what made Joseph and Daniel stand out as God's men was the fact that they could interpret dreams better than all the magicians and evil spiritists of the day. Similarly, we, as Christians in this age, are the ones who should understand the spiritual realm.

Creative Power

We are discussing the flow of spiritual substance from within man. Remember that the spirit of man originated with the breath of God. This is what the Bible teaches. There is some of this *God stuff* in every human being.

It has power to create. Not only does spiritual energy quicken a person's thoughts, allow them to live, influence the natural and spiritual worlds, reach through space and time, govern dreams, etc., but it also releases creative forces. In Volume II, Chapter 10, we compared the spirit of a man with God's Spirit as He brooded over the earth before the creative acts to follow. In similar fashion, the human spirit flows to that which a person envisions. The brooding spirit molds, prepares, and, to some degree, brings into being that which is believed.

Add to our understanding now the concept often used in the Bible, but somewhat concealed by our translation of the Greek word, *phrone* (pronounced, frō nā). This word and its derivatives are translated in several different ways by those who gave us our Bible in our own language. Often it is translated as the *mind-set* of a person (e.g., Rom. 8:5-7; Phil. 3:19; Matt. 16:23). Other times it is translated: *right mind, sensible,* or *sound mind* (e.g., Mark 5:15; Rom. 12:3; II Cor. 5:13; Titus 2:6; I Peter 4:7). In other verses it is not translated with an emphasis on the mind of a person, but on the feelings and attitudes of an individual being directed in a specific way (e.g., Phil. 1:7; 2:5; 3:15).

What we want to see here is that we have no word in our language which communicates fully the meaning of this Greek word, *phrone.* It refers to more than the thought processes, feelings, or attitudes of a person. It is a term referring to the entire orientation of a person's emotions, purpose, affections, thoughts, and heart. We are being exhorted in Bible verses which use this word to orient our entire being toward God, toward others, toward sound judgment, toward the Spirit, etc.

The Greek word *phrone* has the same root meaning as our word *prone.* As a person is prone to do something, they will have a tendency or an inclination to do that very thing. So, also, we should *phrone* our lives toward godly goals and purposes.

One of the most powerful ways we *phrone* our lives is through the visions we have within us. That which we envision orients our thoughts and desires. As we *phrone* in a specific manner, the spiritual energy within us flows out toward the related goals (Vol. II, Chapter 10).

In addition to guiding the visions within one's mind, one of the most effective ways to govern a person's heart and spirit is to ask questions. As we learned, it is the spirit of man which knows and searches the mind of man. Therefore, the spirit of a person instantly responds to the questions placed before that individual.

For this reason, a wife who asks her husband what he did during his day at work really is reaching for his heart. If he shares the things upon his mind, he is redirecting his heart and spiritual energy toward her.

The questions we ask ourselves are equally as powerful in orienting our own heart. A medical researcher who spends hours and days in the lab searching for answers is aiming his spirit at the problems before him. An inventor who designs new things in his mind is working with the creative energy which God placed within man. A philosopher who meditates on the unsolved mysteries of life is pointing his spirit at the dilemmas facing society.

This power of man's spirit also can be used negatively. Of course, people may use the creative forces within to invent, design, plan, and develop new ways to carry out evil deeds. It is equally as true that an individual may use the spiritual energy within himself *against himself.*

To see this, picture a man who has recurring memories of some failure in his past. He only will be adding power to those memories if, in his own mind, he repeatedly asks himself questions such as, "Why am I always having these memories?" or "Why was I so stupid to do that?" or "When will these memories go away?" Such questions only direct the spirit more forcefully upon the memory and thus empower it. It is like digging a hole deeper and deeper while standing in that hole.

Instead, the man in our example should ask himself questions such as, "Does God love me anyway?" or "Didn't Jesus die to forgive me?" or "Does not God love me right now?" As a person answers, "Yes," to such questions, he is *"phroneating"* his heart toward God.

Another example is of the person who constantly focuses on his own inabilities. By *"phroneating"* in such a fashion, he will give those weaknesses greater power. On the other hand, he may learn to change the orientation of his life by asking himself questions such as, "Will God help me?" "Does God want me to succeed?" and "Can I do all things in Christ Jesus?" As he learns to answer these questions in the affirmative, he will aim his spiritual energy toward success.

A person who trains himself to ask the right questions within his own mind will have amazing authority over his own life. Every person constantly is formulating thoughts within his own mind. As he asks himself questions concerning God, life, self, the world, or anything else, his spirit immediately searches for the answer. In addition, his spirit flows out accordingly attempting to touch the spiritual and natural worlds to bring forth the required circumstances, provisions, and events. Therefore, a person who asks himself the right questions is governing his spirit—and remember—the one who rules his spirit is greater than he who rules a city (Prov. 16:32).

A final question worth our attention here is, "To what degree can the *phroneated* heart/soul/ spirit actually influence the physical realm?"

We do not want to imply that man can create as completely or wonderfully as God does. In no way are we placing man on an equal level with God. Rather, we simply are identifying how man was created in the image of God. As we made the comparison in Volume II, a toy airplane is made in the image of a real airplane. Similarly, man is made in the image of, but not equal to, God.

Of course, there are greater creative forces released when many people are in unity, all *"phroneated"* the same. For this reason, God declared over the united people who were building the tower of Babel: "Nothing which they purpose to do will be impossible for them" (Gen. 11:6). Because of this collective authority, people working in unity can accomplish greater feats than an individual working alone.

Scientists endeavoring to discover new facts about the universe around us will accelerate their research if they learn to relate to one another and share their insights. The people working at NASA, all working toward successfully traveling into outerspace, will feed off of each others' spiritual strength and ignite new thoughts in each other. A team of professional businesspeople has the potential to put together a much more effective business plan than one person by himself. A football team that is bonded one to another can function as a unit and win many more games.

Even one individual by himself has powerful forces flowing from within. Jesus said that he who believes could order a mountain to move and it would obey (Mark 11:23). This implies tremendous potential in the supernatural ability of even a single person.

How much power does one person have? We already discussed how some things will not change, no matter how much people believe. (An insane person who believes they are a bird will not be able to fly, no matter how convinced they are that they can fly.) But let's *phroneate* ourselves to answer the question, "Can a person change his own physiological makeup to any degree by what he believes about himself?"

Consider a person who suffers from a schizophrenic disorder. He believes that he is one person at one time and then another person at a different time. What is fascinating is how his physical body may change, to some degree, according to the personality which he is manifesting. For example, a schizophrenic person may have serious allergies in one personality, while in another personality there is absolutely no evidence of those allergies. Other schizophrenics require eye glasses, yet have perfect vision while in another personality. Similarly, some show illnesses such as diabetes in one personality and no sign of this disease while in another personality. Actual physical and biochemical changes can be observed with these personality changes

It is not only the seriously disturbed person who influences his bodily functions. What every person believes to some degree influences his own metabolic rates, immune system responses, secretion of hormones, and countless other physiological conditions..

Do such changes actually reach into the cellular makeup of a person? Can they reach even into the molecular level? Can faith even change the DNA in a human being?

Since our Lord taught that even mountains can be moved by our faith, certainly we have to conclude that the smallest particles can and will be changed by our faith.

Realize that the human body is a changing, flowing, evolving entity rather than a stagnant structure. It is a fact that millions of cells are sloughed off the human body every day. New cells constantly are being produced every second. There is not one cell in your body today that will be there seven years from today. Because there is a constant exchange of new for old, it is accurate to think of the human body as a slow-moving river constantly in motion. Notice that this is just like the spiritual side of man. As the rivers of spiritual energy continually flow from within man, so, also, is the natural flowing outward.

What does this mean if the DNA code of a person changes? If one cell changes, it will reproduce that change over and over again. Of course, we are proposing DNA changes that are only slight over the course of many years—yet real.

Not only can a person gradually be altered in his physiological makeup, but the genetic code he passes on to his descendants may be altered also. Yes, the beliefs, goals, desires—the *phrone*—of a person will alter the course of generations to follow.

To some, this may sound like evolutionary thought. Please do not judge this on the basis of "it sounds like." In Volume VI, entitled, *The Nature of Creation*, we will discuss more fully how living things grow and change. For now, all we are teaching is that people do change—spiritually, soulishly, and physically—according to what they believe. The spirit of a man, indeed, does form that man. As a man thinks within himself, so he is (Prov. 23:7).

Conclusion

The spirit of man influences both the natural and spiritual worlds. We have discussed related subjects such as the spiritual presence of a person, the emanation of his spirit, the power behind spoken words, out-of-body experiences, how the spirit senses through space and time, the function of dreams, and the creative forces within man.

These topics may seem too mystical or too "far out" for some people. In many Christian circles today these topics are taboo, and others simply avoid speaking publicly about them because they stir up unwanted controversy. By God's grace, we trust that the biblical understanding which we have developed will benefit the Body of Christ.

At this time in history our discussion of these subjects is essential. God is raising the Church to a place of maturity and power. We are moving in a direction, and that direction is advancement.

Each time God advances His people in some area, He begins by inspiring related teachings. In the Book of Amos we are told:

> Surely the Lord God does nothing
> Unless He reveals His secret counsel
> To His servants the prophets (Amos 3:7).

Before God acts in significant ways, He stirs the leaders of His people to begin teaching and speaking on the related subjects. As John the Baptist was sent to prepare the way of the Lord, God inspires various leaders to begin speaking out the plans of God, before He acts.

For example, before Christians began speaking in tongues, there was much teaching being brought forth on the subject. Today, most of the Body of Christ are aware of this gift, and even if they do not use it personally, they recognize Christians who do. The point is that God will stir leaders to teach on a subject before and during His release of that specific gift.

We are teaching on the whole realm of the supernatural because it is time for the Church to enter into a greater experience of God's power and provision. It is not just the exercise of tongues that we need. In the Bible we read about people seeing into the spiritual realm, having angelic visitations, perceiving the future, interpreting dreams, being led by the Holy Spirit, experiencing the glory of God, etc. God desires to open His Church to greater dimensions of the spiritual realm. Therefore, we speak, and we will continue advancing in the volumes which follow this one.

Developing a Prosperous Soul
Vol. I: How to Overcome a Poverty Mind-set
Vol. II: How to Move into God's Financial Blessings

There are fundamental changes you can make in the way you think which will release God's blessings. This is a balanced look at God's promises with practical steps you can take to move into financial freedom. It is time for Christians to recapture the financial arena.

Spiritual Realities
(Now five volumes* of a seven volume series)
Here they are—the series explaining the spiritual world from a Christian perspective. In this series Harold R. Eberle deals with issues such as:

- What exists in the spiritual world   - How people access that realm
- Discerning things in the spirit   - Out-of-the-body experiences
- Interpretation of dreams   - What the dead are experiencing
- Angelic and demonic visitations
- Activities of witches, psychics and New Agers
- The Christian perspective of holistic medicine
- Spiritual impartations and influences between people
- Understanding supernatural phenomena from a Biblical perspective

Now you can have answers to the questions you always have wanted to ask about the supernatural world and spiritual phenomena.

Vol. I: The Spiritual World and How We Access It
Vol. II: The Breath of God in Us
Vol. III: Escaping Dualism

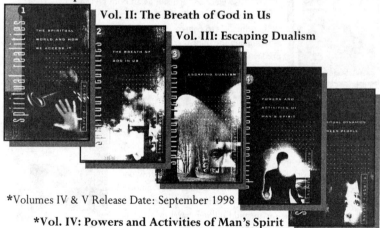

*Volumes IV & V Release Date: September 1998
*Vol. IV: Powers and Activities of Man's Spirit
*Vol. V: Spiritual Dynamics Between People

People Are Good

Harold R. Eberle is stirring up controversy with this one. Furthering the present reformation within the Church this book will cause a major paradigm shift in your mind. It will challenge fundamental beliefs, yet set Christians free and rejoicing. After reading this book you will look at life differently—more positively, with more hope and more realistically. You never will be the same.

You Shall Receive Power

Moving Beyond Pentecostal & Charismatic Theology
God's Spirit will fill you in measures beyond what you are experiencing presently. This is not about Pentecostal or Charismatic blessings. There is something greater. It is for all Christians and it will build a bridge between those Christians who speak in tongues and those who do not. It is time for the whole Church to take a fresh look at the work of the Holy Spirit in our individual lives. This book will help you. It will challenge you, broaden your perspective, set you rejoicing, fill you with hope, and leave you longing for more of God.

Dear Pastors and Traveling Ministers,

Here is a manual to help pastors and traveling ministers relate and minister together effectively. Topics are addressed such as finances, authority, ethical concerns, scheduling,.... In addition to dealing with real-life situations, an appendix is included with very practical worksheets to offer traveling ministers and local pastors a means to communicate with each other. Pastors and traveling ministers can make their lives and work much easier simply by reading this manual.